# TEMPLE WORSHIP

# TEMPLE WORSHIP

## 20
### TRUTHS THAT WILL
### BLESS YOUR LIFE

ANDREW C. SKINNER

DESERET
BOOK

SALT LAKE CITY, UTAH

**Library of Congress Cataloging-in-Publication Data**

Skinner, Andrew C., 1951-
   Temple worship : 20 truths that will bless your life / Andrew C. Skinner.
      p.   cm.
   Includes bibliographical references and index.
   ISBN-13: 978-1-59038-805-1 (hardback : alk. paper)
   1. Mormon temples.   2.  Temple endowments (Mormon Church)  3.  Worship.
I. Title.
   BX8643.T4S55 2007
   264'.09332—dc22                                                         2007033627

Printed in the United States of America
Publishers Printing, Salt Lake City, UT

10   9    8    7    6    5    4    3    2    1

# CONTENTS

CONTENTS

# ACKNOWLEDGMENTS

Nothing of worth in my life has ever happened without the help of heaven, loved ones, friends, and scholars. Nothing I have ever written has found its way into print without the assistance of many individuals. In the writing of this volume on the blessings and doctrinal truths of our temple worship, I have had superior help.

To my wife, Janet, goes my everlasting appreciation for her insights, her patience as I wrote, and her example. She shows our family what it means to put the lessons learned from her temple worship into practice. She is my confidante and companion in every way. I thank my children, especially Cheryl, Mark, and Suzie, for asking questions about the temple that helped clarify my thinking.

I thank my professional assistant at the Neal A. Maxwell Institute for Religious Scholarship at Brigham Young University, Alison Coutts, for her help in the creation of the manuscript. I have prevailed on her good graces too often, and yet she has remained cheerful without fail. Her gospel scholarship, editorial expertise, and efficiency have been a blessing. As usual, thanks likewise go to Connie Lankford Brace, my secretary for many years at BYU, for her watchful eye, which has also helped to guide this project to completion. She and her husband are dear friends. I also thank our student secretary at the Neal A. Maxwell Institute, Elin Jenson, for reading the manuscript and offering suggestions as well as encouraging words.

Last but not least, I thank my friends at Deseret Book Company for their help and encouragement. Cory Maxwell is a gentleman and a scholar. He is perhaps the most patient and positive professional in the publishing industry. Suzanne Brady has been my editor and my good friend for more years than either one of us will admit to outsiders. She is everything an author needs in an editor.

# INTRODUCTION: REFLECTIONS ON THE TEMPLE

This volume touches on truths that we may glean from our experiences in the house of the Lord and which can bless our lives and strengthen our testimonies. Obviously it is not comprehensive. It does not teach in detail about what happens in the temples of the Lord but, rather, discusses the doctrines and principles on which temple worship is founded and the blessings that flow from temple worship. It came about as the culmination and convergence of several developments.

More than a decade ago, I began thinking intensely about statements made by Hugh Nibley regarding the temple. He had said profound things, truths that have become a part of me, my own thoughts and my own words, though their exact expressions are original with him.[1] The temple is a model of the universe; the temple represents "the principle of ordering the universe"; the temple is where we get our bearings regarding our place in the universe; the temple was and is the center of civilization, or, as Professor Nibley said, "There is no part of our civilization which doesn't have its rise in the temple"; the temple is a tangible symbol of the principle of eternal progression which culminates in godhood; the temple reflects things as they exist in heaven—things as they really are; the temple is where heaven and earth intersect; the temple gives us an eternal perspective on life's challenges; and the temple is the place where eternity becomes reality, where "time, space, and lives are extended."[2]

In fact, our English word *temple* comes from the Latin *templum* and means "a sacred space," marked out for the observation of the heavens. In the ancient Roman worldview, the heavens were the place where signs and portents originated and from where the gods answered humans. A temple was a place where sacred things took place involving gods and mortals.

Professor Nibley's insights became all the more profound to me while I was researching and writing about the Dead Sea Scrolls. In particular, I reflected seriously on the beliefs and practices of the Essenes, who were likely the covenanters living in the Dead Sea Scrolls community of Qumran.[3] The texts and practices that riveted my attention, and continue to do so, are those that touch on the temple.

The scrolls indicate that the members of the Qumran community regarded themselves as true Israel surrounded by spiritual traitors and false brethren in a corrupt world. A principal theme of the Dead Sea Scrolls concerns the community awaiting the advent of certain messiahs from their wilderness habitation, where apostasy and persecution had driven them. They believed the Jerusalem temple had become defiled by the corrupt priesthood serving there. The basic ideal for the covenant makers at Qumran was to live as though they were in the midst of the temple itself, every minute of every day. They sought to make their isolated community an open-air temple, and they wore white linen robes to symbolize the level of temple-like purity they sought to attain.

Of special interest among the Dead Sea Scrolls is the Temple Scroll found in Cave 11 at Qumran. It is the longest of the scrolls—twenty-seven feet of parchment (leather) sheets stitched together—and purports to record the words of God to Moses. The text describes an ideal temple to be established by God himself at the end of days (last days) and that temple's connection with the covenant God made with Jacob at Bethel. Says God: "And I will consecrate my Temple by my glory, [the Temple] on which I will settle my glory, until the day of the blessing [or, the day of creation] on which I will create my Temple and establish it for myself at all times, according to the covenant which I have made with Jacob at Bethel."[4]

This passage caught my attention when I first read it because of Latter-day Saint prophetic commentary on Jacob's covenant at Bethel. In a powerful discussion entitled "Temples—The Gates to Heaven," President Marion G. Romney seems to have implied that the events at Bethel recorded in Genesis 28 constituted Jacob's endowment:

> Pondering upon the subject of temples and the means
> therein provided to enable us to ascend into heaven brings
> to mind the lesson of Jacob's dream. You will recall that in

3

the twenty-eighth chapter of Genesis there is an account of his return to the land of his father to seek a wife from among his own people. When Jacob traveled from Beersheba toward Haran, he had a dream in which he saw himself on the earth at the foot of a ladder that reached to heaven where the Lord stood above it. He beheld angels ascending and descending thereon, and Jacob realized that the covenants he made with the Lord there were the rungs on the ladder that he himself would have to climb in order to obtain the promised blessings—blessings that would entitle him to enter heaven and associate with the Lord.

Because he had met the Lord and entered into covenants with him there, Jacob considered the site so sacred that he named the place Bethel, a contraction of Beth-Elohim, which means literally "the House of the Lord." He said of it: " . . . this is none other but the house of God, and this is the gate of heaven." (Gen. 28:17.)

Jacob not only passed through the gate of heaven, but by living up to every covenant he also went all the way in. Of him and his forebears Abraham and Isaac, the Lord has said: " . . . because they did none other things than that which they were commanded, they have entered into their exaltation, according to the promises, and sit upon thrones, and are not angels but are gods." (D&C 132:37.)

Temples are to us all what Bethel was to Jacob.[5]

This stunning statement makes the Old Testament come alive to Latter-day Saints and causes us to be impressed with the importance placed on the temple by the covenant makers at Qumran. Though we have no indication that the Qumran community regarded their ideal future temple described in the Temple Scroll as anything more than an Aaronic priestly edifice, albeit in a pure and uncorrupted form, they understood the significant connection between covenants, Israel, and the temple. And their belief system bears witness to the truth that the temple was the center of their community.

The capstone to my ponderings during this time regarding the importance of the temple to societies, ancient and modern, came when Elder Carlos E. Asay, an emeritus member of the Seventy, spoke to the Religious Education faculty at Brigham Young University about the temple. He was then serving as the president of the Salt Lake Temple. He said many marvelous and inspiring things that stirred my soul in ways that have never left me.

President Asay told us that when he and his wife had been set apart by President Gordon B. Hinckley as president and matron of the Salt Lake Temple, the prophet charged them to be advocates of temple activity. He said President Hinckley taught the importance of the temple when he "commanded" them to speak about temple attendance "at all times and in all things, and in all places that ye may be in" (using the language of the baptismal covenant in Mosiah 18:9).

Not only had he and his wife been true to their commission, President Asay said, but they had sometimes been accused of becoming "overly zealous" in their work. He then said with great power, "We would rather be true to a prophet's commission than be acceptable to those who become tinged with guilt whenever the House of the Lord is mentioned."[6]

He went on to talk about some of the blessings and applications of temple attendance that he thought might be worthy of serious consideration. Consider some of the subheadings of his address:

"The Blessings of an Examined Life"

"The Blessings of Participation in Perfect Pedagogy"

"The Blessings of Being Perfected in an Understanding of Our Ministries"

"The Blessings of the Holy Endowment"

"The Blessing of Walking on the Bridge That Spans Heaven and Earth"

"The Blessing of Taking Away from the Temple Precious Teachings, Feelings, and Resolves"

President Asay, this good man who had spent a lifetime in the service of the Lord, was culminating that service by presiding in the Salt Lake Temple. He delivered his message with such power that when I walked out of that meeting, four unequivocal truths were confirmed in my mind:

1. The temple is the ultimate place of covenant-making activity.
2. The temple is the ultimate place of learning in mortality.
3. The temple is truly where heaven and earth, time and eternity, God and man come together.
4. The promises found in the temple are what I crave for myself, my family, and my friends.

This volume, then, is in some ways the tangible result of

the reflections of the past decade, when for me things began to point to the temple as the place of ultimate blessings and the most important place on earth. Perhaps all of us get caught up at one time or another in the thick of thin things, but I believe that when we're reminded of the blessings and realities of eternity as only the temple can remind us, our sights are lifted, we refocus on what matters most, and the Spirit of the Lord teaches us things known only to Deity. My hope is that this book will increase our desire to attend the temple more often so we can avail ourselves of that divine teaching.

# 1

## THE ULTIMATE EXPRESSION OF OUR WORSHIP

*What takes place in Latter-day Saint temples is the
ultimate expression of our worship.*

The ordinances administered [in the temple] represent
the ultimate in our worship. These ordinances become
the most profound expressions of our theology," said
President Gordon B. Hinckley. "I urge our people everywhere, with all of the persuasiveness of which I am capable,
to live worthy to hold a temple recommend, to secure one
and regard it as a precious asset, and to make a greater effort
to go to the house of the Lord and partake of the spirit and
the blessings to be had therein."[1]

The Lord's people in every age have been commanded to
worship him: "Thou shalt worship the Lord thy God, and
him only shalt thou serve" (Matthew 4:10). The ultimate
place and way to worship is found in the temples of the Lord.
This truth was understood by the Saints in Nauvoo, Illinois,
where modern temple worship in the more complete sense
really began. The Saints were desperate to participate in that

9

form of worship before they set out for the American West, an exodus comparable only to that of ancient Israel's departure from Egypt. Elder Russell M. Nelson noted an important parallel between ancient Israel and the Saints in Nauvoo: "The children of Israel had a portable tabernacle wherein covenants were made and ordinances were performed to strengthen them on their journey. Many Latter-day Saints were endowed in the Nauvoo Temple before their arduous trek westward."[2]

The temple is a place where the Lord's people have always gone to be fortified, strengthened, and blessed before the performance of arduous, challenging, difficult tasks. It was so in the past; it is so today. The temple is the ultimate place of refuge and blessing. So anxious were the Nauvoo Saints to participate in temple worship before they set out that they worked intensely, almost frantically, to complete the work of building the temple and to receive the ordinances within it.

On November 30, 1845, seventeen months after the martyrdom of Joseph and Hyrum Smith, Brigham Young and twenty other individuals who had received their own temple ordinances from Joseph Smith assembled and dedicated the attic floor of the Nauvoo Temple for ordinance work. For the next ten days they prepared this attic "council chamber" for the presentation of the endowment ordinance. The area was divided by canvas partitions, each section representing a phase, or stage, of man's eternal progress in God's plan of salvation and happiness. Church members throughout the city contributed fine furnishings for these areas, the most beautiful being placed in the area symbolizing the celestial kingdom. When Joseph Fielding entered this part of the temple for the first time, he felt he had truly "gotten out of the World."[3]

The first presentation of the endowment in the Nauvoo Temple was on December 10. Participation by the Saints was constant over the next several weeks. On Christmas Day alone, 107 persons received their endowment. By the end of the month, more than 1,000 Church members had participated in that ordinance. As 1846 began and pressure for the Saints to leave Nauvoo increased, so too did the yearning of the Saints to participate in temple ordinances and receive the powers and blessings of heaven before facing the unknown. On January 12, Brigham Young recorded: "Such has been the anxiety manifested by the saints to receive the ordinances [of the Temple], and such the anxiety on our part to administer to them, that I have given myself up entirely to the work of the Lord in the Temple night and day, not taking more than four hours sleep, upon an average, per day, and going home but once a week."[4]

On January 21, 1846, the number of endowment ordinances administered on a single day exceeded 200 for the first time. The pace of temple worship intensified as February 4, the day appointed for departure from Nauvoo, approached. On February 3, 1846, Brigham Young again recorded:

> Notwithstanding that I had announced that we would not attend to the administration of the ordinances, the House of the Lord was thronged all day, the anxiety being so great to receive, as if the brethren would have us stay here and continue the endowments until our way would be hedged up, and our enemies would intercept us. But I

informed the brethren that this was not wise, and that we should build more Temples, and have further opportunities to receive the blessings of the Lord, as soon as the saints were prepared to receive them. In this Temple we have been abundantly rewarded, if we receive no more. I also informed the brethren that I was going to get my wagons started and be off. I walked some distance from the Temple supposing the crowd would disperse, but on returning I found the house filled to overflowing. Looking upon the multitude and knowing their anxiety, as they were thirsting and hungering for the word, we continued at work diligently in the House of the Lord.[5]

On that day, February 3, nearly 300 persons participated in the endowment. In the eight-week period before the exodus from Nauvoo, approximately 5,500 individuals received the endowment ordinance. Temple worship had become temple work.

The question this stirring episode naturally evokes is, Why were the Saints so anxious to receive the ordinances of the house of the Lord, and why were the leaders so anxious to administer them? It is precisely because the ultimate in our worship as Latter-day Saints occurs within the walls of the structures that have been dedicated as the house of the Lord, the place where his presence can and does reside. He is no absentee landlord. As Elder Erastus Snow testified of those hectic days just before the Saints left Nauvoo, "The Spirit, Power, and Wisdom of God reigned continually in the Temple and all felt satisfied that during the two months we occupied it in the endowments of the Saints, we were amply paid for all our labors in building it."[6]

The temple represents the ultimate in our worship

because ordinances are performed and covenants made therein that cannot be done anywhere else on earth. "Temple ordinances and covenants teach of the redeeming power of the Atonement," said Elder Nelson.[7] In the temple things are said relative to the Atonement that should not be uttered anywhere else on earth. Sacred things, especially the particulars of the Atonement and the principles of eternal life that flow from it, should not be cheapened. They must be protected. President Boyd K. Packer said:

> The ordinances and ceremonies of the temple are simple. They are beautiful. They are sacred. They are kept confidential lest they be given to those who are unprepared. Curiosity is not a preparation. Deep interest itself is not a preparation. Preparation for the ordinances includes preliminary steps: faith, repentance, baptism, confirmation, worthiness, a maturity and dignity worthy of one who comes invited as a guest into the house of the Lord.[8]

Even though the Nauvoo Saints had their temple for only eight weeks in which to receive their endowments, they felt it was worth all the effort—all the blood, sweat, toil, and tears—because it gave them the ultimate worship experience. It blessed their lives beyond mortal measure, and it will bless ours as well. As the Lord revealed through the Prophet Joseph Smith, all who "enter upon the threshold of the Lord's house may feel [his] power . . . and receive a fulness of the Holy Ghost" (D&C 109:13, 15). That is a stunning promise, one reserved for the elect—those who "harden not their hearts" (D&C 29:7).

The phrase "fulness of the Holy Ghost" is unique in scripture, occurring only in Joseph Smith's prayer dedicating the Kirtland Temple. It reflects something of the Prophet's special feeling for the temple. Of this phrase, President Brigham Young said, "If the Latter-day Saints will walk up to their privileges . . . and live in the enjoyment of *the fulness of the Holy Ghost* constantly day by day, there is nothing on the face of the earth that they could ask for, that would not be given to them."[9] He indicates that to enjoy the "fulness of the Holy Ghost" is ultimately to "possess all things." Such is the result of sincere and constant temple worship.

We will consider other reasons why the Prophet Joseph Smith was so focused on the temple and why he said toward the end of his life, "We need the temple more than anything else."[10] To begin to do that, we must examine what we know about our premortal existence in relation to the temple.

# 2

## THE PROMISE OF
## ETERNAL LIFE

*In our premortal existence, our Father in Heaven,
the Great Parent of the universe, promised eternal
life to all his spirit children who work for it—
a truth confirmed in the temple.*

That the being we sometimes refer to as Elohim is literally our Father is a truth beyond question. He is the
Father of our spirit bodies, our spirit beings, the real you and
me. Long ago, the apostle Paul taught this truth in plainness:
"Furthermore we have had fathers of our flesh which cor-
rected us, and we gave them reverence: shall we not much
rather be in subjection unto the Father of spirits, and live?"
(Hebrews 12:9).

In speaking of the Fatherhood of God, the First
Presidency of The Church of Jesus Christ of Latter-day
Saints (Joseph F. Smith, John R. Winder, and Anthon H.
Lund) issued a statement in November 1909 entitled "The
Origin of Man." They boldly declared: "All men and women
are in the similitude of the universal Father and Mother and

are literally the sons and daughters of Deity. 'God created man in His own image.' This is just as true of the spirit as it is of the body, which is only the clothing of the spirit, its complement—the two together constituting the soul. The spirit of man is in the form of man, and the spirits of all creatures are in the likeness of their bodies."[1]

Other prophets have taught that God the Father is the supreme parent of the universe, that if we do not understand the nature and character of God, we do not comprehend ourselves, that as God's offspring we human beings have the potential to become as he is, and that we may speak with God as child to parent—all of which the Prophet Joseph Smith discussed powerfully in his King Follett discourse:

> God himself . . . is an exalted man, and sits enthroned in yonder heavens! That is the great secret. If the veil were rent today, and the great God who holds this world in its orbit, and who upholds all worlds and all things by his power, was to make himself visible,—I say, if you were to see him today, you would see him like a man in form—like yourselves in all the person, image, and very form as a man; for Adam was created in the very fashion, image and likeness of God, and received instruction from, and walked, talked and conversed with him, as one man talks and communes with another. . . . It is the first principle of the Gospel to know for a certainty the Character of God, and to know that we may converse with him as one man converses with another.[2]

As the supreme Father and Ruler of the universe, God is all-powerful (Alma 26:35) and all-knowing (Alma 26:35; 2 Nephi 9:20). He answers the prayers of all his children, according to their faith (2 Nephi 26:15; Mosiah 21:15;

Mormon 9:37). He cares for all of his children with a love so profound that finite mortal minds cannot comprehend it, though we receive significant reminders of it in the temple.

Indeed, love is the core attribute of God's perfect character and makeup. This is the meaning, I think, of John's declaration "For God is love" (1 John 4:8). The attribute of perfect love influences, shapes, and mediates all of the Father's other qualities. "For with all the other excellencies in his character, without this one to influence them, they could not have such powerful dominion over the minds of men; but when the idea is planted in the mind that he is love, who cannot see the just ground that men of every nation, kindred, and tongue, have to exercise faith in God so as to obtain eternal life?"[3]

In 1986, President Gordon B. Hinckley bore his witness of the reality of God the Father, of his perfect character and attributes, and summarized the principles we have been discussing, which are taught in the temple.

I believe without equivocation or reservation in God, the Eternal Father. He is my Father, the Father of my spirit, and the Father of the spirits of all men. He is the great Creator, the Ruler of the Universe. He directed the creation of this earth on which we live. In His image man was created. He is personal. He is real. He is individual. He has "a body of flesh and bones as tangible as man's" (D&C 130:22). . . .

. . . I worship Him "in spirit and in truth." I look to Him as my strength. I pray to Him for wisdom beyond my own. I seek to love Him with all my heart, might, mind, and strength. His wisdom is greater than the wisdom of all men. His power is greater than the power of nature, . . . His love is greater than the love of any other, for His love encompasses all of His children, and it is His work and His glory to bring to pass the immortality and eternal life of His sons and daughters of all generations (see Moses 1:39).[4]

Perhaps the greatest manifestation of the Father's love and concern for his children is his concentrated focus on extending to his sons and daughters the same powers and blessings he enjoys. "For behold, this is my work and my glory—to bring to pass the immortality and eternal life of man" (Moses 1:39). As Joseph Smith taught, all who desire it, pray for it, and work for it "shall be heirs of God and joint heirs with Jesus Christ. What is it? To inherit the same power, the same glory and the same exaltation, until you arrive at the station of a God, and ascend the throne of eternal power, the same as those who have gone before."[5]

So it is that the apostle Paul testified to the ancient Church of Jesus Christ that eternal life was the ultimate promise God gave to his spirit sons and daughters in premortality. "Paul, a servant of God, and an apostle of Jesus Christ, according to the faith of God's elect, and the acknowledging of the truth which is after godliness; in hope of eternal life, which God, [who] cannot lie, promised before the world began" (Titus 1:1–2). This powerful text is not an obscure one. It has been available to every reader of the Bible down through the ages.

The foundation of all that happens in Latter-day Saint temples is based on this fundamental, premortal promise made by God and repeated by the great apostle to the Gentiles in the first century, Paul of Tarsus. It is a great blessing to know that our Father in Heaven has put in place an unchanging promise of exaltation to every son or daughter who desires it. It is a great blessing to know that God has the power and knowledge to fulfill his premortal promises. This temple teaching becomes an anchor to us, giving us security and comfort in the midst of life's trials, tragedies, temptations, and tests. We can withstand much if we know that our Father in Heaven can and will make everything right in the end. It is a great blessing to understand our true relationship to God. It is a great blessing to understand the nature of our premortal existence, as taught in the temple. Because of our Heavenly Father's premortal promise of eternal life, *all* who enter the temple may bask in his love and tender mercies.

# 3

## ORDINANCES AND COVENANTS

*All ordinances and covenants pertaining*
*to eternal life were instituted by the Father and*
*the Son before the world was created.*

God not only promised eternal life to his offspring in pre-mortality but also established the ordinances and covenants by which eternal life could be obtained. This truth is confirmed by modern prophets as well as in the Lord's modern-day temples. The Prophet Joseph Smith taught that "God himself, finding he was in the midst of spirits and glory, because he was more intelligent, saw proper to institute laws whereby the rest could have a privilege to advance like himself."[1]

The concept of God's instituting laws, ordinances, and covenants in premortality to lead his children to eternal life became a theme to which the Prophet Joseph Smith returned again and again. In April 1842, he taught that Jehovah, the premortal Christ, also knew and taught in our premortal existence the doctrine of required ordinances for eternal life:

The great Jehovah contemplated the whole of the events connected with the earth, pertaining to the plan of salvation, *before it rolled into existence,* or ever "the morning stars sang together" for joy; the past, the present, and the future were and are, with Him, one eternal "now"; He knew of the fall of Adam, the iniquities of the antediluvians, of the depth of iniquity that would be connected with the human family, their weakness and strength, their power and glory, apostasies, their crimes, their righteousness and iniquity; He comprehended the fall of man, and his redemption; He knew the plan of salvation and pointed it out; He was acquainted with the situation of all nations and with their destiny; He ordered all things according to the council of His own will.[2]

On July 12, 1843, the Prophet recorded one of the greatest revelations of this, or any, dispensation regarding the new and everlasting covenant, including the eternal covenant of marriage. Quoting the Lord, he referred to the premortal nature of the ordinances and covenants on which the plan of redemption and happiness is based:

> For all who will have a blessing at my hands shall abide the law which was appointed for that blessing, and the conditions thereof, as were instituted from before the foundation of the world. . . .
>
> Behold, mine house is a house of order, saith the Lord God, and not a house of confusion.
>
> Will I accept of an offering, saith the Lord, that is not made in my name?
>
> Or will I receive at your hands that which I have not appointed?
>
> And will I appoint unto you, saith the Lord, except it be

by law, even as I and my Father ordained unto you, before the world was? (D&C 132:5, 8–11)

On October 9, 1843, Joseph Smith again emphasized the premortal origin of the ordinances of eternal life. "If men would acquire salvation, they have got to be subject, before they leave this world, to certain rules and principles, which were fixed by an unalterable decree before the world was."[3] When the Prophet says men must be subject to certain rules and principles *before* they leave this world, he is obviously referring to those who have the opportunity to learn of them in mortality.

Allowance has been made by the Father and the Son for those who die before a knowledge of the ordinances and covenants of eternal life could be imparted to them. This aspect of the Father's plan was not an afterthought, though it did not become operational until after Jesus' mortal death on the cross and his redemptive sojourn in the world of spirits (see D&C 138). The doctrines and ordinances pertaining to the redemption of the dead were also instituted in our premortal existence. Said the Prophet Joseph Smith, "You may think this order of things to be very particular; but let me tell you that it is only to answer the will of God, by conforming to the ordinance and preparation that the Lord ordained and prepared before the foundation of the world, for the salvation of the dead who should die without a knowledge of the gospel" (D&C 128:5).

President Brigham Young also revealed the establishment of saving ordinances during our premortal existence. When speaking about baptism, for example, he stated: "What is required of us as soon as we come to the years of accountability? It is required of us, for it is an institution of heaven, the origin of which you and I cannot tell, for the simple reason that it has no beginning, it is from eternity to eternity—it is required of us to go down into the waters of baptism."[4] There is no question that the ordinances of exaltation were established long before this earth was formed and revealed to us in these latter days.

The establishment of temples in this dispensation is based on revelation—the revelation of matters pertaining to our premortal condition, the promises made there, the ordinances outlined there, and the building of temples here to administer those ordinances. President John Taylor asked: "Whoever thought of building Temples until God revealed it? . . . And did you know how to administer in them after they were built? No, you did not."[5] All this has been done according to revelation. Elder Bruce R. McConkie of the Quorum of the Twelve Apostles said: "The inspired erection and proper use of temples is one of the great evidences of the divinity of the Lord's work. . . . Where there are temples, with the spirit of revelation resting upon those who administer therein, there the Lord's people will be found; where these are not, the Church and kingdom and the truth of heaven are not."[6]

Without doubt, the temple is the great symbol of the Lord's kingdom and our membership in it. But it also seems to me that the temple is the great symbol of the foreordained plan of exaltation. Temples are a parallel to patriarchal blessings and a complement to them. Both outline the course and direction the Lord charted for us in our premortal existence. Both are intricately tied to revelation. One is a corporate experience (involving many members at a time); the other is a very private and personal experience (involving only the Lord, the patriarch, and the individual). Both are designed to reveal our path back to the Father. The connection between temples and patriarchal blessings is strong. There are times in our lives—sometimes in the company of others, sometimes alone—when heaven whispers to us that we are understood and loved and attended to by the Great Parent of the universe. Temples provide a sanctified environment for that to happen.

It is a great blessing to enter the Lord's temple and come to know that God our Father comprehended the end from the beginning and that his hand is over his children (Abraham 2:8). He knew all things pertaining to the salvation of humankind before they occurred. His plan includes every contingency. All things were prepared for, and every one of his children accounted for. The learning that occurs in the Lord's holy house ultimately confirms that God has been in charge since before time began. He knew each of us individually and personally before this earth was formed. The Father is not a novice; he is not surprised by anything that happens or will happen. He is not a grand technician who must check the manuals when some new twist turns up in our lives or in our prayers. He is mighty to save because he possesses all power and all knowledge, *and* all laws, ordinances, and covenants issue from him. He "hath given a law unto all things" (D&C 88:42), and "he is above [ruler of] all things" (D&C 88:41). This is one of the great comforts we take away from our experience in the temple: God's promises to us are sure and certain.

# 4

## ESSENTIAL ORDINANCES OF SALVATION

*All individuals must obey the very same plan of
salvation and obtain eternal life by the same principles and
ordinances instituted before the world was created; full
salvation cannot be obtained without these ordinances.*

In April of 1842, the Prophet Joseph Smith described the
perfect fairness of God when he said, "God will deal with
all the human family equally."[1] Without doubt, all people
are treated the same by God. The Book of Mormon teaches
that the Savior "inviteth them [the children of men] all to
come unto him and partake of his goodness; and he denieth
none that come unto him, black and white, bond and
free, male and female; and he remembereth the heathen;
and all are alike unto God, both Jew and Gentile" (2 Nephi
26:33).

Perhaps the most famous illustration of this principle
comes from the early Church, specifically the ministry of the
chief apostle, Peter (see Acts 10:1–11:24). On a particular
day he received a vision at high noon, a time when it could

not be dismissed as a bad dream, that completely obliterated a practice of discrimination among the Jews of Peter's day. Peter was told that those who were being called unclean or untouchable—namely, the Gentiles—were not only acceptable to God but were now to be sought out by Church leaders. Peter then taught the gospel of Jesus Christ to Cornelius, a Gentile, who became the first person we know of in that dispensation to convert to Christianity without first having to subscribe to Judaism. Out of this watershed experience came Peter's famous declaration: "Of a truth I perceive that God is no respecter of persons" (Acts 10:34).

Indeed, God does not play favorites; he denies no one, and all of his children are alike in his view. In February 1979, at a fourteen-stake gathering on the campus of Brigham Young University in Provo, then-Elder Howard W. Hunter delivered an address entitled "All Are Alike unto God." He emphasized the truth that the Father's plan "transcends nationality and color, crosses cultural lines, and blends distinctiveness into a common brotherhood."[2] The opportunities are the same for all individuals because "we are all of one blood and the literal spirit offspring of our eternal Heavenly Father."[3]

Undoubtedly, some will say that this does not always seem to have been the case. Frankly, I do not have an answer for every seeming exception in the past, but we are told that Deity will explain all things to us some day (see D&C 121:26–32) and put right all that has gone wrong. In the meantime, I know that we possess the mind and will of the Lord for our day. No one is prevented from enjoying the blessings that the gospel of Jesus Christ has to offer. Just as important is the corollary, which is also true: No one may join the Church, no one may enjoy the blessings of the gospel, no one may be exalted without receiving the same foreordained covenants and ordinances as everyone else. The Prophet Joseph was clear and certain about this matter:

> Ordinances instituted *in the heavens before the foundation of the world,* in the priesthood, for the salvation of men, are not to be altered or changed. *All must be saved on the same principles.* . . . One of the ordinances of the house of the Lord is baptism for the dead. *God decreed before the foundation of the world* that that ordinance should be administered in a font prepared for that purpose in the house of the Lord. . . .
>
> If a man gets a fullness of the priesthood of God he has to get it in the same way that Jesus Christ obtained it, and that was by *keeping all the commandments* and obeying all the ordinances *of the house of the Lord.* . . .
>
> All men who become heirs of God and joint heirs with Jesus Christ *will have to receive the fulness of the ordinances of his kingdom;* and those who will not receive all the ordinances will come short of the fullness of that glory, if they do not lose the whole. [4]

All individuals are exalted by the very same priesthood power and priesthood ordinances. There are no exceptions. Thus, this requirement applies to the dead as well as to the living. Joseph Smith declared, "Every man who wishes to save his father, mother, brothers, sisters and friends, *must go through all the ordinances* for each one of them separately, the same as for himself, from baptism to ordination, washing and anointings, and receive all the keys and powers of the Priesthood, *the same as for himself.*"[5]

The Prophet seems to have encountered some opposition to this doctrine, for in 1844 he said: "The question is frequently asked, 'Can we not be saved without going through with all those ordinances?' I would answer, No, not the fulness of salvation . . . and any person who is exalted to the highest mansion has to abide a celestial law, and the whole law too."[6]

This statement is significant for more than one reason. It emphasizes the universal nature of God's requirements for salvation, but it also confirms that there are different degrees of salvation. The fulness of salvation is exaltation, encompassing the whole range of God's laws, ordinances, and blessings—or what the Doctrine and Covenants calls the law of the celestial kingdom. As the Lord tells us, if we are not able to comply with all the laws and ordinances that govern the celestial kingdom and that help us to become pure and holy, we cannot (and would not want to) live in the environment of the celestial glory: "That bodies who are of the celestial kingdom may possess it forever and ever; for, for this intent was it made and created, and for this intent are they sanctified. And they who are not sanctified through the law which I have given unto you, even the law of Christ, must inherit another kingdom, even that of a terrestrial kingdom, or that of a telestial kingdom" (D&C 88:20–21).

God is not whimsical, requiring some things from one person but a little more or a little less from another. That is precisely one powerful message of the temple. No one is better than another. As President James E. Faust said: "Fundamental to temple worship is the principle that 'God is no respecter of persons.' Within the hallowed walls of the temples, there is no preference of position, wealth, status, race, or education."[7]

I repeat, no one is above another in the temple because of race, or skin color, or political affiliation, or wealth, or opportunities for learning. It *is* true that the righteous are "favored," or blessed, by God over the unrighteous (1 Nephi 17:35). But no one is denied opportunities or privileges for any reason except choosing to disobey the commandments. All must make the same covenants and receive the same ordinances. No exceptions and no privileges! All will be blessed.

Sometimes we hear it said that life isn't fair. True enough, I suppose. But we never have to worry about that being true in the temple. All is fair, and all are equal—which we naturally expect if the temple really is the home of the Lord (and, of course, it is). So important is this status of equality before the Lord that in the temple all are dressed alike. That is, every sister wears white clothing, the same as every other sister; every brother wears white clothing, the same as every other brother.

"White is the symbol of purity," said Elder John A. Widtsoe. "No unclean person has the right to enter God's house. Besides, the uniform dress symbolizes that before God our Father in heaven all men are equal. The beggar and the banker, the learned and the unlearned, the prince and the pauper sit side by side in the temple and are of equal importance if they live righteously before the Lord God."[8]

From his own experience, Elder Russell M. Nelson of the Quorum of the Twelve Apostles provides a masterful lesson about equality in the temple: "In the temple, all are dressed in spotless white. 'The symbolic purity of white like-wise reminds us that God is to have a pure people.' Age, nationality, language—even position in the Church—are of secondary significance. I have attended many endowment sessions when the President of the Church participated. Every man in the room was accorded the same high regard that was extended to the President. All sit side by side and are considered equal in the eyes of the Lord. Through a democracy of dress, temple attendance reminds us that 'God is no respecter of persons.'"[9]

It is significant that the holiest spot on earth, the place where heaven and earth intersect, strongly reaffirms our equal status before God the Father and his Son Jesus Christ. All are alike unto God. Temple clothing is a symbol not only of purity but also of equality. I can say without hesitation that some of my happiest, most contented moments have come while seated in the temple observing my wife, my children, and other family members dressed in white, equal before the Lord. And then I think I do not have to wait to know what the celestial kingdom will be like because I have already glimpsed it.

# 5

## PRIESTHOOD POWER AND PRIESTHOOD ORGANIZATION

*Priesthood power and priesthood organization have*
*always existed; they constitute the authority to administer*
*all the ordinances of exaltation.*

The Prophet Joseph Smith taught that the "priesthood is an everlasting principle, and existed with God from eternity, and will to eternity, without beginning of days or end of years. . . . The Priesthood is everlasting."[1] President Joseph Fielding Smith made it clear that priesthood power and priesthood organization existed among the Father's children before any of us came to this earth as mortal beings. In a 1966 general conference address he said: "With regard to the holding of the priesthood in the preexistence, I will say that there was an organization there just as well as an organization here, and men there held authority. Men chosen to positions of trust in the spirit world held the priesthood."[2] Thus, in the temple when we learn about such leaders as Peter, James, and John carrying out assignments while only Adam and Eve inhabited this newly formed earth, they could do so with perfect propriety, holding priesthood authority, because the priesthood was organized and functioning in pre-mortality, before any of us were born into our second estate. The temple reflects reality.

The prophetic statements of Joseph Smith and Joseph Fielding Smith help us better understand the teachings of Alma on the foreordination of priesthood holders:

> And again, my brethren, I would cite your minds forward to the time [we would say "back toward the beginning"] when the Lord God gave these commandments unto his children; and I would that ye should remember that the Lord God ordained priests, after his holy order, which was after the order of his Son, to teach these things unto the people.
>
> And those priests were ordained after the order of his Son, in a manner that thereby the people might know in what manner to look forward to his Son for redemption.
>
> And this is the manner after which they were ordained—being called and prepared from the foundation of the world according to the foreknowledge of God, on account of their exceeding faith and good works; in the first place being left to choose good or evil; therefore they having chosen good, and exercising exceedingly great faith, are called with a holy calling, yea, with that holy calling which was prepared with, and according to, a preparatory redemption for such. (Alma 13:1–3)

Here we learn three important facts:

First, God is ultimately in charge of the priesthood, and he oversees its delegation to others, determining who is ordained ("God ordained priests, after his holy order"; v. 1). In this sense, the Prophet Joseph Smith taught, "All the prophets had the Melchizedek Priesthood and were ordained by God himself."[3]

Second, the Lord God called and prepared Melchizedek Priesthood holders "from the foundation of the world" (that is, before any of the Father's children entered mortality) on account of their faith and good works in our first estate.

Third, all things in our premortal existence were done in accord with a preparatory redemption. That is to say, the atonement of Jesus Christ already operated on our behalf in premortality in preparation for our mortal sojourn. His infinite and eternal atonement—meaning it was effective both before and after mortality—made it possible for us to enter mortality without stain or guilt, unmarred, born with a clean slate, so to speak. The Lord put it more powerfully: "Every spirit of man was innocent in the beginning; and God having redeemed man from the fall, men became again, in their infant state, innocent before God" (D&C 93:38). From the beginning of mortal life on this earth, it was revealed that the atonement of Jesus Christ operated from the "foundation of the world" (Moses 6:54; see also 7:47).

Not only did the Prophet Joseph Smith teach about the eternal nature of the priesthood and its operation in our premortal existence, but he also taught that the priesthood administers all covenants and ordinances pertaining to our full salvation or exaltation: "The keys [of the priesthood] have to be brought from heaven whenever the Gospel is sent. . . . Wherever the ordinances of the Gospel are administered, there is the Priesthood."[4] Temple ordinances are administered under the direction of the Melchizedek Priesthood. In fact, the ordinances, promises, and blessings of exaltation administered in the temple are called the fulness of the Melchizedek Priesthood, as President Ezra Taft Benson told us: "To enter into the order of the Son of God is the equivalent today of entering into the fulness of the Melchizedek Priesthood, which is only received in the house of the Lord."[5]

It cannot be emphasized too strongly that *only* in the temple can we become entitled to the blessings of the fulness of the priesthood, as President Joseph Fielding Smith stated: "I do not care what office you hold in this Church—you may be an apostle, you may be a patriarch, a high priest, or anything else—you cannot receive the fulness of the priesthood unless you go into the temple of the Lord and receive these ordinances. . . . No [one] can get the fulness of the priesthood outside of the temple of the Lord."[6] But the fulness of the priesthood *is* available to anyone who is worthy to enter the house of the Lord.

There is no exaltation in the kingdom of God without the fulness of the priesthood. Thus, the fulness of the priesthood might also be termed the keys of exaltation. President Smith established this equivalency:

"Only in the temple of the Lord can the fulness of the priesthood be received. Now that temples are on the earth, there is no other place where the endowment and the sealing powers for all eternity can be given. No man [or woman] can receive the *keys of exaltation* in any other place."[7] Only the Melchizedek Priesthood is the power by which men and women can enter our Heavenly Father's presence or, as the Doctrine and Covenants puts it, "see the face of God, even the Father, and live" (D&C 84:22). It is not surprising, therefore, that the first revelation of this dispensation recorded in the Doctrine and Covenants (given September 21, 1823) promises a restoration of a significant portion of the priesthood: "Behold, I will reveal unto you the Priesthood, by the hand of Elijah the prophet, before the coming of the great and dreadful day of the Lord" (D&C 2:1).

President Benson asked, "What priesthood was Elijah to reveal? John the Baptist restored the keys to the Aaronic Priesthood. Peter, James, and John restored the keys of the kingdom of God. Why send Elijah?" He then answered his own question with these significant words:

> "Because he [Elijah] holds the keys of the authority to administer in all the ordinances of the priesthood," or the sealing power. (*Teachings*, p. 172.) So said the Prophet Joseph Smith!
>
> The Prophet Joseph said further that these keys were "the revelations, ordinances, oracles, powers and endowments of the fulness of the Melchizedek Priesthood and of the kingdom of God on the earth." (*Teachings*, p. 337.)
>
> Even though the Aaronic Priesthood and Melchizedek Priesthood had been restored to the earth, the Lord urged the Saints to build a temple to receive the keys by which this order of priesthood could be administered on the earth again, "for there [was] not a place found on earth that he may come to and restore again that which was lost . . . even the fulness of the priesthood." (D&C 124:28.) . . .
>
> So the Kirtland Temple was completed at great sacrifice to the Saints.
>
> Then, on 3 April 1836, the Lord Jesus Christ and three other heavenly beings appeared in this holy edifice. One of these heavenly messengers was Elijah, to whom the Lord said

he had "committed the keys of the power of turning the hearts of the fathers to the children, and the hearts of the children to the fathers, that the whole earth may not be smitten with a curse." (D&C 27:9.)

Elijah brought the keys of sealing powers—that power which seals a man to a woman and seals their posterity to them endlessly, that which seals their forefathers to them all the way back to Adam. This is the power and order that Elijah revealed.[8]

The Prophet Joseph Smith taught that there is a lineal order to priesthood authority. "Christ is the Great High Priest; Adam next,"[9] he said. Known in premortality as Michael the Archangel, Adam was the first mortal to hold priesthood authority on this earth. He held the keys of the First Presidency. Next in authority to Adam, third from Jesus Christ, is Noah (who is Gabriel). He "was the father of all living in this day."[10] Whenever the keys of the priesthood— the right of presidency, which is the power to direct the use of priesthood authority—are "revealed from heaven, it is by Adam's authority."[11] Thus, Elijah, who held the same priest-hood as Noah and Adam, restored the sealing powers under Adam's direction as well as the Lord's. That is why the Lord said to Joseph Smith, "For verily I say unto you, the keys of the dispensation, which ye have received, have come down from the fathers, and last of all, being sent down from heaven unto you" (D&C 112:32).

What an incomparable blessing to know that the sealing powers, which constitute the fulness of the Melchizedek Priesthood, are used every day by those holding this power and are available to us, almost at our beckoning, in the temples of the Lord. It is striking to realize that Joseph Smith was consumed by temple matters until the day he died. As late as April 1842, he urged, "The Church is not fully organized, in its proper order, and cannot be, until the Temple is completed, where places will be provided for the administration of the ordinances of the Priesthood."[12] That is the same perspective and sense of urgency we get from President Gordon B. Hinckley. In 1996 during a seminar for new temple presidents and matrons, he said, "Without temples and temple activity, we would have only half a church."[13]

In truth, that is the state and condition of the rest of Christianity, which lacks temples of the Lord. And it makes our message even more compelling. How blessed are the Latter-day Saints. How grateful and humble that should make us feel. How much more motivated we should be to encourage others to join the Church and to help all members to prepare to enter the house of the Lord, especially members of our own families. In the words of President Ezra Taft Benson, given at the centennial commemoration of the Logan Temple: "God bless Israel! . . . God bless us to teach our children and our grandchildren what great blessings await them by going to the temple. God bless us to receive all the blessings revealed *by Elijah the prophet* so that our callings and election will be made sure."[14]

God be thanked for the marvelous gift of temples and the fulness of the priesthood found therein. What a sense of peace, security, and continuity will be conveyed to our children, grandchildren, nieces and nephews, as we teach them these truths. What a sense of appreciation will be engendered in them for the Prophet of the Restoration,

Joseph Smith, the man who gazed into eternity and brought those visions within our view.

We have now come full circle to the point at which we began. Priesthood power and organization operated in our premortal existence. We were taught there that God's own power—the priesthood, which includes the sealing power—would be made available to men and women in mortality. These are eternal powers and eternal principles. We come to understand them and value them only as we participate in temple worship. Let us go to the temple and claim the blessings of eternity our Heavenly Father is offering to us.[15]

# 6

## THE ATONEMENT OF
## JESUS CHRIST

*All of the foreordained principles and ordinances of the
Father's plan, especially those received in the temple, are
intricately tied to the Atonement of Jesus Christ.*

The atonement of Jesus Christ is the most important
event in time or all eternity. Nothing ever has or ever
will compare in importance to the redemption provided by
Jesus Christ, who was God (Jehovah) come-to-earth. All
other things "which pertain to our religion are only
appendages to it [the Atonement]."[1] It is only natural that
the holiest place on earth, the temple, would be grounded in
and centered on the Atonement. Elder Russell M. Nelson
taught us that "temple ordinances and covenants teach of
the redeeming power of the Atonement."[2]

The atonement of Jesus Christ ransoms and redeems all
of creation from the effects of sin, death, hell, and the devil.
Physical and spiritual death are answered. Christ redeems
all that he creates, which is "worlds without number"
(Moses 1:33). Joseph Smith recast this doctrine, originally

articulated in Doctrine and Covenants 76:22–24, 40–43, in magnificent poetic form:

> And I heard a great voice bearing record from
>     heav'n,
> He's the Saviour and Only Begotten of God—
> By him, of him, and through him, the worlds were all
>     made,
> Even all that career in the heavens so broad.
> Whose inhabitants, too, from the first to the last,
> Are sav'd by the very same Saviour of ours;
> And, of course, are begotten God's daughters and
>     sons,
> By the very same truths, and the very same
>     pow'rs.[3]

The temple ceremony teaches all participants that the redemption provided by the Savior was no afterthought but rather the core of our Heavenly Father's plan for his children. Temple teachings parallel a statement by the Prophet Joseph Smith that the plan of exaltation was established around the appointment of Jesus Christ as our Savior and Redeemer in premortality: "The first step in the salvation of man is the laws of eternal and self-existing principles. . . . At the first organization in heaven we were all present, and saw the Savior chosen and appointed and the plan of salvation made, and we sanctioned it."[4]

This is not a new or strange doctrine. Ancient apostles clearly understood it. For example, Paul wrote to the Ephesian Saints: "Blessed be the God and Father of our Lord Jesus Christ, who hath blessed us with all spiritual blessings in heavenly places in Christ: according as he hath chosen us in him before the foundation of the world, that we should be holy and without blame before him in love: having predestinated us unto the adoption of children by Jesus Christ to himself, according to the good pleasure of his will" (Ephesians 1:3–5).

Often we dismiss Paul's use of the word *predestinated* (Greek, *proorizdo*, "decide from the beginning or before-hand"). But, in fact, it is the right word here. Although no one is predestined or predetermined to receive exaltation or eternal condemnation before being born into mortality, the vehicle of our exaltation, the Atonement, *was* predestined. That is to say, all who are eventually exalted, based on choices they make in mortality, are predestined to be exalted through the atonement of Christ and in no other way: "And moreover, I say unto you, that there shall be no other name given nor any other way nor means whereby salvation can come unto the children of men, only in and through the name of Christ, the Lord Omnipotent" (Mosiah 3:17). Remember, King Benjamin taught this doctrine at least 120 years *before* Jesus entered mortality.

The Prophet Joseph Smith confirms our understanding of this aspect of the Atonement: "God did elect or pre-destinate, that all those who would be saved, should be saved in Christ Jesus."[5] Thus, one aspect of the concept of predestination is true doctrine.

The power, efficacy, and reality of Jesus Christ's atone-ment were never in doubt. Put another way, the redemptive effects of the Atonement were guaranteed; our acceptance of it, our commitment to it, our behavior, were not. There is never any sense conveyed in the temple that the Atonement was a shaky proposition. Rather, it is understood to be the rock-solid foundation of eternity. The Father knew the end from the beginning. He knew the infinite goodness and loyalty of his Only Begotten Son. He foreknew and foresaw the actual suffering of his Son in Gethsemane's garden and on Golgotha's cross eons before they were a physical reality on earth. It was never a questionable happening. In addition, we know that Jesus was already a god in premortality, and his sojourn in mortality would not change his standing.

One ramification of this profound doctrine is that the ordinances of exaltation, including their general symbolism and specific tokens centering on the bodily sacrifice of Christ were in place and likely foreknown by us in our premortal existence. Another ramification is that the Atonement, as we have already indicated, was in operation—its power already in effect—during our premortal existence. Consider the following verses, which describe the atonement of Christ as being operative from the foundation of the world:

> And behold, Enoch saw the day of the coming of the Son of Man, even in the flesh; and his soul rejoiced, saying: The Righteous is lifted up, and the Lamb is *slain from the foundation of the world*; and through faith I am in the bosom of the Father, and behold, Zion is with me. (Moses 7:47; emphasis added)
>
> And all that dwell upon the earth shall worship him, whose names are not written in the book of life of the Lamb *slain from the foundation of the world.* (Revelation 13:8; emphasis added)
>
> And our father Adam spake unto the Lord, and said: Why is it that men must repent and be baptized in water? And the Lord said unto Adam: Behold I have forgiven thee thy transgression in the Garden of Eden.

Hence came the saying abroad among the people, that the Son of God hath atoned for original guilt, wherein the sins of the parents cannot be answered upon the heads of the children, for they are whole *from the foundation of the world.* (Moses 6:53–54; emphasis added)

The passage from Moses 6 specifically declares that forgiveness of Adam's transgression was provided by the Savior's atonement, even though most of the human family, including the Savior, were still living in our premortal estate. Though not carried out physically until Jehovah became the mortal Jesus in the Holy Land, it was as if the physical event of Jesus' atoning sacrifice had already occurred. Prophecy was as history in reverse. The Savior's sacrifice was the predetermined vehicle of our redemption.

If the Atonement was in operation during our premortal existence, then, does that mean sin was to be found during that phase of our existence? It certainly seems possible. Elder Orson Pratt, writing about the nature of sin in our premortal existence, said that "among the two-thirds [of God's spirit children] who remained, it is highly probable that, there were many who were not valiant . . . , but whose sins were of such a nature that they could be forgiven through faith in the future sufferings of the Only Begotten of the Father, and through their sincere repentance and reformation. We see no impropriety in Jesus offering Himself as an acceptable offering and sacrifice before the Father to atone for the sins of His brethren, committed not only in the second, but also in the first estate."[6]

Is it possible that the reason one-third of the Father's children were cast out of his presence for rebellion is that they ultimately and finally refused to accept not just the role of Jesus as our Redeemer but also the means by which their rebellion could have been forgiven, namely the atonement of Jesus Christ, which was operative in our premortal existence? Perhaps.

Personal, probing reflection on the temple ceremony teaches us that in our premortal existence we possessed an extensive knowledge of our Savior's selfless offer of redemptive suffering as well as the ramifications of his atonement. But there is much more. The connection between the temple and the Atonement is *not* tenuous or weak on any level. When we go to the temple and participate in the required, foreordained covenants and ordinances of exaltation on behalf of our deceased ancestors or on behalf of anyone who has passed on to the spirit world, we are acting as the Savior himself acted—providing a vicarious service for those who could not and cannot now participate in those ordinances and covenants as mortal beings. These ordinances and covenants must be accomplished with a physical, mortal body. Thus, as Elder David B. Haight of the Quorum of the Twelve Apostles noted, regular temple worship "is one of the simplest ways you can bless those who are waiting in the spirit world."[7] But more than that, when we "provide the sacred ordinances of the temple for [our] ancestors . . . [we] will know the indescribable joy of being a savior on Mount Zion to a waiting ancestor."[8]

This magnificent concept was taught by Elder D. Todd Christofferson in this way: "The principle of vicarious service should not seem strange to any Christian. In the baptism of a living person, the officiator acts, by proxy, in place of the Savior. And is it not the central tenet of our faith that Christ's sacrifice atones for our sins by vicariously satisfying the demands of justice for us? As President Gordon B. Hinckley has expressed: 'I think that vicarious work for the dead more nearly approaches the vicarious sacrifice of the Savior Himself than any other work of which I know. It is given with love, without hope of compensation, or repayment or anything of the kind. What a glorious principle.'"[9] I repeat, we are never more like the Savior than when we minister to the deceased through vicarious service in the temple, doing for others that which they cannot do for themselves. This is the very essence of the Savior's life.

Temple worship, including vicarious service for the deceased, is the premier expression of our belief in the power and infinite reach of the atonement of Jesus Christ. Temple worship testifies of our sure knowledge of many aspects of the Atonement: "First, of Christ's Resurrection; second, of the infinite reach of His Atonement, third, that He is the sole source of salvation; fourth, that He has established the conditions for salvation; and fifth, that He will come again."[10]

The teachings found in the temple are like a funnel. They begin broadly, focusing our attention ever more narrowly on the Son of God and his atoning activities in mortality. Temple teachings also pull together principles from different dispensations in a dramatized, step-by-step ascent to godhood, always with the Atonement in mind.

Sometimes we are surprised to find reflections of the temple in the words of ancient prophets. Isaiah, for example, saw in prophetic vision the Savior's atoning sacrifice and surely had His crucifixion in mind as he referred to one *Eliakim* (Hebrew name meaning "God shall cause to arise") who was fastened as "a nail in a sure place" (Isaiah 22:23).

But our surprise turns to grateful appreciation when we realize that these glimpses reflect a perfect, established plan, with
temples as an integral part of that plan. Temples of the Lord
and what goes on inside them are the Lord's great gift for the
dispensation of the fulness of times. They are also a symbol
of that dispensation, our dispensation, when God promised
to "gather together in one all things *in Christ*" (Ephesians
1:10; emphasis added). That is one reason why Christ is at
the center of latter-day temples and temple work. All things
in this last dispensation are connected to him.

# 7

## THE RICHEST GIFTS
## ON EARTH

*Temples are where the richest gifts*
*on this earth are given.*

A rich gift is often referred to as an endowment. The richest gift our Father in Heaven can bestow on his children is eternal life: "The mysteries of God shall be unfolded unto you, and then shall you be made rich. Behold, he that hath eternal life is rich" (D&C 6:7). Within the sacred precincts of the temple, Deity endows, or gives to, all who are worthy the knowledge and power necessary to enable them to obtain eternal life. The presentation of this knowledge and power is the temple endowment. In fact, however, the temple endowment itself is also a representation of the actual endowment, which is eternal life. The presentation of the endowment in the temple culminates in the symbolic bestowal of eternal life in the celestial kingdom upon the worthy participants. The temple endowment, then, is among other things a presentation, a representation, and a symbol. It points us to the ultimate gift of eternal life and gives to us what we need to obtain it.

The Prophet Joseph Smith said, "You need an endowment . . . that you may be prepared and able to overcome all things."[1] In a sense, eternal life is the overcoming of all things, including all the obstacles that the adversary (the Hebrew word *satan* means "adversary") throws in our path. The Lord provides what we need to overcome all things through his divine program of learning. The keystone of that divine program is a righteous home; the temple is the capstone.

The temple endowment is not a casual matter, nor was it intended to be understood fully in one or two visits to the temple. President David O. McKay is reported to have said, after nearly sixty years of temple attendance: "Now I am beginning to understand the endowment."[2] If it took a prophet of God of the spiritual depth of President McKay almost six decades to begin to understand the temple endowment, I think we may be pardoned if we sometimes don't understand—but only if we approach our deficiency in a spirit of humility and resolve to do better. President McKay also said, "There are few, even temple workers, who comprehend the full meaning and power of the temple endowment."[3] Of course, the lesson in this is that if any of us wants to begin to "plumb the depths of this godly mystery,"[4] as President Asay called it, we must go often to the temple with a seeking mind and heart.

Because the temple endowment is complex as well as sacred, several Church leaders have illuminated various aspects of it. President Brigham Young's oft-quoted definition is a helpful starting point: "Your endowment is, to receive all those ordinances in the House of the Lord, which are necessary for you, after you have departed this life, to enable you to walk back to the presence of the Father, passing the angels who stand as sentinels, being enabled to give them the key words, the signs and tokens, pertaining to the holy Priesthood, and gain your eternal exaltation in spite of earth and hell."[5]

Perhaps some of the language in President Young's description is figurative and some literal. I do not know how much actual walking is involved in returning to the Father's presence; however, I take very seriously and very literally the requirement of "key words, the signs and tokens, pertaining to the holy Priesthood" and of being able to present them to the Gatekeeper. Nonetheless, in connection with President Young's statement, I am persuaded that prophets of God know and have seen much more than they usually say as they give us glimpses of eternity until we are prepared to receive more.

Another helpful insight regarding the temple endowment was offered by Elder James E. Talmage, who referred to it as a "course of instruction . . . relating to the significance and sequence of past dispensations, and the importance of the present as the greatest and grandest era in human history."[6] President McKay added a complementary insight: "Seen for what it is, [the endowment] is the step-by-step ascent into the Eternal Presence."[7] The word *sequence* in Elder Talmage's description is meaningful as we ponder the dramatized sweep and flow of events associated with salvation history on this earth, as presented in our temples. The phrase "step-by-step ascent" used by President McKay is literally borne out in some architectural features of modern temples. For example, the baptismal font used for proxy baptisms is physically, or spatially, lower than the area representing this earth and mortal life. That area in turn is spatially lower than the celestial room, which represents the celestial kingdom and the presence of the Father and the Son, and is where the culminating experience of the presentation of the endowment occurs.

President Boyd K. Packer provided this succinct comment on the nature of the temple endowment: "To endow is to enrich, to give to another something long lasting and of much worth. The temple endowment ordinances enrich in three ways: (a) The one receiving the ordinance is given power from God. 'Recipients are endowed with power from on high' (b) A recipient is also endowed with information and knowledge. 'They receive an education relative to the Lord's purposes and plans' (*Mormon Doctrine*, 277) (c) When sealed at the altar a person is the recipient of glorious blessings, powers, and honors as part of his endowment."[8]

In truth, the temple endowment encompasses all of these aspects spoken of by prophetic commentators. The endowment is preparatory (involving all ordinances necessary to make us ready to lay hold on eternal life); it is a course of instruction; it is a step-by-step ascent to God's presence; and it is an enrichment of power given by God to mortals.

The temple endowment is presented in stages. The early stages include washings, anointings, and receipt of sacred, symbolic clothing. The late Hugh Nibley of Brigham Young University documented significant and amazing parallels between these ordinances and initiation rituals (and their now-lost meanings) in ancient civilizations, especially Judaism and Christianity. In other words, Professor Nibley demonstrated clearly that the modern temple ordinances composing the endowment were not invented by Joseph

Smith, nor did he know of their precedents or antecedents in history.

Professor Nibley noted, for example, that according to the ancient Christian writer-theologian Cyril, washings were an initiation into immortality. Cyril said ritual washing was followed "by an anointing, making every candidate, as it were, a messiah. The anointing of the brow, face, ears, nose, breast, etc. represents 'the clothing of the candidate in the protective panoply of the Holy Spirit' which however does not hinder the initiate from receiving a real GARMENT on the occasion. . . . Furthermore, according to Cyril, the candidate was reminded that the whole ordinance is 'in imitation of the sufferings of Christ,' in which 'we suffer without pain by mere imitation [of] his receiving of the nails in his hands and feet.'"[9] We need to remember that this account is that of an ancient writer speaking of the nature of special ordinances as he knew them.

Citing a statement by Rabbi Akiba, a revered Jewish leader of late antiquity, Professor Nibley also called to our attention the fact that "the Jews once taught that Michael and Gabriel will lead all the sinners up out of the lower world: 'they will wash and anoint them, healing them of their wounds of hell, and clothe them with beautiful pure garments and bring them into the presence of God' [said Rabbi Akiba]."[10]

Other examples from ancient history and religious texts regarding endowment-like ceremonies abound, including the practice of special washings, anointings, and clothing the initiates or participants in ritual garments. Let us consider four more.

The first comes from an intertestamental text catalogued by scholars as part of the Old Testament Apocrypha and Pseudepigrapha and entitled Second Enoch. The Apocrypha and Pseudepigrapha are sets of ancient, scripture-like writings not regarded as authoritative and therefore not included in our biblical canon. Through revelation the Prophet Joseph Smith indicated that those enlightened by the Holy Spirit may obtain some benefit from reading these texts (D&C 91:1–6). The passage from Second Enoch reads:

> And the Lord, with his own mouth, called to me, "Be brave, Enoch! Don't be frightened! Stand up, and stand in front of my face forever." And Michael, the Lord's greatest archangel, lifted me up and brought me in front of the face of the Lord. . . . The Lord said to Michael, "Take Enoch, and extract (him) from the earthly clothing. And anoint him with the delightful oil and put (him) into the clothes of [my] glory." And Michael extracted me from my clothes. He anointed me with the delightful oil; . . . And I gazed at all of myself, and I had become like one of the glorious ones. (2 Enoch 22:5, 8–10)[11]

Having been properly endowed, Enoch is now qualified to associate with the exalted ("the glorious ones").

A second example also comes from the Old Testament Pseudepigrapha, in a text called the Apocalypse of Elijah. It is important to remember that the word *apocalypse* is Greek and means "to uncover" or "reveal." That is what the temple endowment is, an uncovering or a revealing of divine, sacred truths in a series of ordinances. This Elijah text reads: "Now those upon whose forehead the name of Christ is written and upon whose hand is the seal, both the small and the great, will be taken up. . . . Then Gabriel and Uriel will become a pillar of light leading them into the holy land. It will be granted to them to eat from the tree of life. They will wear white garments. . . . They will not thirst, nor will the son of lawlessness be able to prevail over them" (Apocalypse of Elijah 5:5–6).[12] Elements of this text sound as if they were plucked from the Book of Mormon. Not only is the motif of eating from the tree of life familiar to us (see 1 Nephi 11 concerning partaking of Christ's atonement) but also the idea of a holy land, or a promised land, as a symbol for eternal life, which we may enter by following our spiritual Liahona or compass (see Alma 37:38–45). It is also significant that this endowment text is associated with Elijah, the prophet who held and restored the keys of the sealing power.

A third example comes from the New Testament Apocrypha and Pseudepigrapha. The text entitled the Gospel of Truth was found among the papyri at Nag Hammadi in Egypt. According to Professor Nibley's reading, "The word of the Father clothes everyone from top to bottom, purifies, and makes them fit to come back into the presence of their Father and their heavenly mother."[13] (Yes, the ancients did believe in a heavenly mother.)

The fourth and final example is, in some ways, the most impressive. Colloquially designated as the Egyptian Endowment Scene, it is a series of panels carved into a stone wall in the huge open-air temple at Karnak, Egypt, on the Nile. The temple complex was built over thirteen hundred years, beginning some time in the second millennium before Christ.

The sequence of the panels from the temple at Karnak shows how the initiation ceremony was conducted. In each scene, the words of the speakers, candidate, and attendants are written at the top of the panel. First, the candidate is washed and anointed. The attendants who escort the candidate stand on either side of him, pouring out vials over the candidate's head. The substance flowing from the vials is represented by the *ankh* hieroglyphic, the term and symbol in ancient Egypt for "eternal life." Next, the candidate is given a crown and, while having the ankh sign touched to his lips, is conducted by the ministers of "life, health, strength, and joy" into the presence of the god Thoth, "who introduces him at the last shrine where he receives the paternal embrace that confirms his appearing in glory 'on the throne of his father [the god], Re.'"[14]

"From the very first . . . the text makes it clear that a real physical embrace took place," says Professor Nibley. Moreover, following the purification ceremony, the candidate "was led by the hand of two gods (priests in masks) . . . to his throne; from there he proceeded to the holy of holies 'to behold his father,' who embraced him and crowned him."[15]

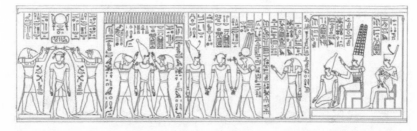

I have stood before this scene in the actual temple in Egypt—which is, of course, much more impressive than the line drawing of the panels reproduced here—and have been overwhelmed by two thoughts. First is the continuity of the elements of the temple endowment over time. Second is the prophetic power possessed by the leaders of this present, and final, dispensation. Our temple endowment was not made up by Joseph Smith, or Brigham Young, or Gordon B. Hinckley, or any mortal. It comes from God.

We are blessed beyond measure to be able to participate in the temple endowment presentation. It is a pattern of things as they have been and are to come. It is symbolic of our Heavenly Father's love. In fact, while serving as president of the Salt Lake Temple, President Carlos E. Asay referred to the endowment as "an exchange of love between God, our Father, and us."[16] He sent his Only Begotten Son out of love (John 3:16). Every commandment, ordinance, covenant, and law is given to us out of love. We as mortals observe and obey these requirements of exaltation out of love. The Savior said, "If ye love me, keep my commandments" (John 14:15). Elder Asay observed: "Yes, the endowment is an exchange of love—divine love. God loves us so he provides us words to live by. We love Him and His Son in return so we enter into covenants and go forward with promises to keep. If we are true to commitments made and the love professed, we draw claim upon blessings that assure us happiness in this life and the prospects of exaltation in the life to come."[17] Given all we learn about the temple endowment, why would we not choose to attend the temple and receive the power to take us into the Father's presence and enjoy eternal life? The temple endowment is the foreordained path to exaltation, to which the ancients gave witness.

# 8

## THE SEALING
## ORDINANCES

*The culminating ordinances of the temple are
those which seal a husband and a wife and children
together as a family for eternity.*

I sat in a sacrament meeting some time ago in which I was captivated by a beautiful eleven-year-old girl who addressed the congregation and boldly but humbly stated in pure tones that she knew she was a daughter of a King. Indeed! We are all daughters and sons of a King—the King of the Universe, who is our Father in Heaven. But more remarkable than this fact is the stunning truth that through his plan, we ourselves may become kings and queens. That is possible through the sealing powers of the priesthood that operate in the temples of our Lord.

Elder Boyd K. Packer wrote that when we participate in the temple endowment, we receive "an investment of eternal potential," which is, in one sense, preliminary and preparatory to our "coming to the altar to be sealed as husband and wife for time and for all eternity." He went on to say that a husband and a wife "become a family, free to act in the creation of life, to have the opportunity through devotion and sacrifice to bring children into the world and to raise them and foster them safely through their mortal existence; to see them come one day, as [we] have come, to participate in these sacred temple ordinances."[1] As we follow this pattern, we are doing what our Heavenly Parents do. We create and nurture life, we provide our sons and daughters with opportunities for growth and progression, and we seek to have them arrive at the point where they desire to continue the pattern, wherein lies true happiness.

Being sealed together as husband and wife and children is not just a nice thing to do, not just the customary pattern to follow. Being sealed together as an eternal family is the very order of heaven. It is the kind of life our Heavenly Parents live. In other words, the family isn't just the basic unit of society; it is the basic unit of eternity.

The sealing power is associated with the fulness of the authority and blessings of the priesthood. Whenever the complete gospel of Jesus Christ has been on the earth, the sealing power has been given by the Lord to his authorized representatives to bind on earth and seal in heaven (Matthew 16:19). When speaking of the ordinances of salvation, generally the sealing power may be regarded as the means whereby "all covenants, contracts, bonds, obligations, oaths, vows, performances, connections, associations, or expectations" are put into full force and operation "after the resurrection from the dead" (D&C 132:7). All things, all relationships and associations, not sealed by this priesthood power "have an end when men are dead" (D&C 132:7).

Elder Bruce R. McConkie wrote of the sealing power as it pertains to temple ordinances: "Unless an eternal marriage covenant is sealed by this authority, it will not take the participating parties to an exaltation [exalted status] in the highest heaven within the celestial world.

"All things gain enduring force and validity because of the sealing power. So comprehensive is this power that it embraces ordinances performed for the living and the dead, seals the children on earth to their fathers who went before them and forms the enduring patriarchal chain that will exist eternally among exalted beings."[2]

In this dispensation, the sealing power is directed by the president of the Church, the senior apostle on earth who holds the keys of the priesthood, a symbolic term meaning the ultimate authority to delegate and direct the use of all priesthood power, including the sealing power. These keys were restored to the earth in two dispensations— the meridian dispensation and our own latter-day dispensation—by the prophet Elijah (see Matthew 17:18; D&C 2:1–3; 110:13–16). "The keys that Elijah held were the keys of the everlasting priesthood, the keys of the sealing power, which the Lord gave unto him. And that is what he came and bestowed upon the heads of Peter, James, and John; and that is what he gave to the Prophet Joseph Smith."[3] Joseph Smith said, "The spirit, power, and calling of Elijah is . . . to hold the key of the revelations, ordinances, oracles, powers and endowments of the fulness of the Melchizedek Priesthood and of the kingdom of God on the earth; and to receive, obtain, and perform all the ordinances belonging to the kingdom of God, even unto the turning of the hearts of the fathers unto the children, and the hearts of the children unto the fathers, even those who are in heaven."[4]

By divine decree, only one man at a time on the earth holds the fulness of the keys of the priesthood, including the sealing power—which is the ultimate power on earth (D&C 132:7). Adam was the first. "The Priesthood was first given to Adam; he obtained the First Presidency, and held the keys of it from generation to generation. . . . The keys have to be brought from heaven whenever the Gospel is sent."[5] In the post-resurrection Church of Jesus Christ, the man to hold the keys was Peter; in 1836 when Elijah appeared in the Kirtland Temple, that man was Joseph Smith; today it is the living prophet and president of The Church of Jesus Christ of Latter-day Saints.

To illustrate this doctrine, Elder Boyd K. Packer recounted a most impressive personal experience. In 1976, after the conclusion of an area conference in Copenhagen, Denmark, he went with President Spencer W. Kimball and other Church leaders to visit the Vor Frue Kirke, the church where Thorvaldsen's statues of the Christus and the Twelve Apostles stand. The Christus stands at the front of the church behind the altar, and the apostles along the sides. Elder Packer recalled:

> Most of the group were near the rear of the chapel, where the custodian, through an interpreter, was giving some explanation. I stood with President Kimball, Elder Rex Pinegar, and President Bentine, the stake president,

before the statue of Peter. In his hand, depicted in marble, is a set of heavy keys. President Kimball pointed to them and explained what they symbolized. Then, in an act I shall never forget, he turned to President Bentine and with unaccustomed sternness pointed his finger at him and said with firm, impressive words, "I want you to tell every Lutheran in Denmark that they do not hold the keys! I hold the keys! We hold the real keys and we use them every day."

This declaration and testimony from the prophet so affected me that I knew I would never forget it—the influence was powerfully spiritual and the impression was physical in its impact as well.

We walked to the other end of the chapel where the rest of the group were standing. Pointing to the statues, President Kimball said to the kind custodian who was showing us the building, "These are the dead Apostles. Here we have the living Apostles." Pointing to me he said, "Elder Packer is an Apostle." He designated the others and said, "Elder Monson and Elder Perry are Apostles, and I am an Apostle. We are the living Apostles. You read about seventies in the New Testament, and here are living seventies, Brother Pinegar and Brother Hales."

The custodian, who to that time had shown no particular emotion, suddenly was in tears. . . . The word *key* is symbolic. The word *sealing* is symbolic. Both represent, I repeat, the consummate authority on this earth for man to act in the name of God.[6]

Thus, the fulness of the authority of the priesthood includes the sealing power. The sealing power is the highest authority and the greatest power on earth. Although Satan is waging an all-out war against righteousness,

especially righteous families on this earth, God's power—
the power of the priesthood—is infinitely greater. The sealing power *will* conquer every enemy: sin, death, hell, and
the devil.

Some aspects inherent in the sealing power of the
priesthood are more perceptible and obvious than others.
One dramatic and visible aspect is control over the elements:
the sealing and unsealing of the heavens and the invocation
and revocation of famine (see 1 Kings 17:1; 18:41–45;
Helaman 10:7; 11:5). Thus, the sealing power gives its pos-
sessor power over all things on earth and the right and ability to have his actions recognized and ratified in heaven by
the Father.[7] It is stunning to realize that the sealing together
of husbands, wives, and children is done by the same power
that seals shut the heavens or changes the elements of the
earth.

Once sealed, husbands, wives, and children are
changed—they belong to each other. In a way we cannot
explain scientifically or even understand completely, the
sealing power welds together a husband, wife, and children
for eternity. The sealing power is a real power in the universe. It affects the physical elements; it changes them,
whether it be the heavens, the weather, the waters and seas,
or the binding together of families. The sealing power, which
is put in force by the Holy Ghost (D&C 132:7), is like the
other powers that are under the control of the third member
of the Godhead. Elder James E. Talmage explained:

> In the execution of these great purposes, the Holy
> Ghost directs and controls the varied forces of nature, of
> which indeed a few, and these perhaps of minor order

wonderful as even the least of them appears to man, have thus far been investigated by mortals. Gravitation, sound, heat, light, and the still more mysterious and seemingly supernatural power of electricity, are but the common servants of the Holy Ghost in His operations. No earnest thinker, no sincere investigator supposes that he has yet learned of all the forces existing in and operating upon matter; indeed, the observed phenomena of nature, yet wholly inexplicable to him, far outnumber those for which he has devised even a partial explanation. There are powers and forces at the command of God, compared with which electricity is as the pack-horse to the locomotive, the foot messenger to the telegraph, the raft of logs to the ocean steamer. With all his scientific knowledge man knows but little respecting the enginery of creation; and yet the few forces known to him have brought about miracles and wonders, which but for their actual realization would be beyond belief. These mighty agencies, and the mightier ones still to man unknown, and many, perhaps, to the present condition of the human mind unknowable, do not constitute the Holy Ghost, but are the agencies ordained to serve His purposes.[8]

An analogy illustrating the kind of force the sealing powers may wield comes from a teaching of the Prophet Joseph Smith. He spoke of the physical effect of the Holy Ghost upon persons who are not literal descendants of Abraham and noted that "as the Holy Ghost falls upon one of the literal seed of Abraham, it is calm and serene . . . while the effect of the Holy Ghost upon a Gentile, is to purge out the old blood, and make him actually the seed of Abraham."[9] In parallel fashion, if the various powers and forces employed by the Holy Ghost can change the nature or characteristics of physical matter, including blood or the elements, surely the effect of the sealing powers upon members of a specific family is more than just metaphorical.

For this reason alone, the sealing powers must be guarded and protected and used only under the direction of the president of the Church. In one sense, we are like children becoming involved with powers and forces we do not fully comprehend. The sealing power is most sacred and its use most serious and solemn.

Another aspect of the sealing power of the priesthood is the ability of the Lord's authorized servant to seal men and women unto eternal life, to perform an ordinance granting them eternal life once they pass beyond mortality, "to place a seal on them so that no matter what happens in the world, no matter what desolation sweeps the earth, yet they shall be saved in the day of the Lord Jesus. (D&C 88:84–85; 109:38, 46; 124:124; 131:5; 132:19, 46, 49)."[10] Elder Bruce R. McConkie added this significant insight: "Since these sealing blessings are conferred by the laying on of hands of those who hold the keys of this power, it follows that John's description of placing a seal in the forehead is not just apocalyptic imagery but a literal description of what takes place. As with other sacred things, however, the devil has a substitute seal to place; he puts a *mark* in the 'foreheads' of his followers also. (Rev. 13:16–18.)"[11]

The sealing of men and women (couples) to eternal life is predicated upon continued faithfulness in mortality over time, *after* their temple marriage, and is not automatic or inherent in the marriage ceremony when a couple is first married in the temple, as temple instruction makes clear. Said President Joseph Fielding Smith, "Blessings pronounced upon couples in connection with celestial marriage are conditioned upon the subsequent faithfulness of the participating parties."[12] In fact, exaltation comes as a result of proven loyalty to the Lord and his kingdom "at all hazards."[13] The Prophet Joseph Smith not only described the kind of complete devotion to righteousness that is required to receive this ultimate blessing but showed us the way.[14] In 1843, after years of serving the Lord at all hazards, Joseph heard the Lord say: "For I am the Lord thy God, and will be with thee even unto the end of the world, and through all eternity; for verily I seal upon you your exaltation, and prepare a throne for you in the kingdom of my Father, with Abraham your father" (D&C 132:49).

Regarding the rest of us, the Lord indicates in Doctrine and Covenants 50:5 that whether such a guarantee comes before death or after mortality has concluded, it makes no difference. The result is the same—exaltation. That is why it is so important for all of us to endure faithfully, patiently, and cheerfully to the end of our mortal lives.

In a way, the temple endowment is preparation for the sealing ordinance of eternal marriage, which in turn is preparation for the promise of eternal life preparatory to the realization of exaltation. The object of this life is more life. And everything we experience in mortality is preparatory for life everlasting. This mortal life really is "*the* time for men to prepare to meet God" (Alma 34:32; emphasis added). And the temple is the great preparer or schoolmaster. Our Heavenly Father's promises all along the way are sure and certain; they give to us increased hope and magnify our faith in a loving Father and a compassionate Son and increase our affection for them.

More than that, great peace, tremendous emotional security, and an increased desire to keep the Lord's covenants come from knowing that the sealing powers are in full operation on our behalf. Think of the comfort that comes to parents and children during times of trial or tragedy in knowing that nothing, whether in heaven or on earth, no person, and no occurrence can break up families who are sealed in the temple for eternity. Only unbridled, unrepented-of rebellion against God on the part of individual family members can do our families any lasting harm. Please permit a personal example.

My parents joined the Church later in their married life, just before I and my sister were born. Several years afterward, when I was ten, we traveled from our home in Colorado to the Salt Lake Temple and were sealed together as a family. I can remember some of the attendant details, but indelibly etched in my mind is the scene of my father and mother, dressed in white, kneeling around an altar, my sister and I at their sides, holding hands with an older woman I did not know. As I found out, she was acting as a proxy. I had forgotten (if I had known at all) that a little girl had been born to my parents between me and the sister with whom I grew up. I was not used to seeing my parents shed tears, but tears flowed freely that day. I came to realize that they were tears of happiness (still one of nature's ironies to me). That feeling of overwhelming happiness was compounded by the sense that everyone else in the temple that day and, later, in our home ward, was truly happy for us.

Four years later, my father died unexpectedly. For days I was inconsolable. Later, family friends told my mother (and me) that for a while they were exceptionally worried about my state. I do remember how bad I felt—until the thought came into my mind one day that we had been sealed as a family. All was not lost if I would try diligently to live as I had been taught. There was still pain, but I could endure it and make sense of it. Those thoughts and feelings about the temple and the sealing power changed my life. Even now, much of the time they are not far from my consciousness. When I returned to the temple, the Salt Lake Temple, in fact, just before I left for full-time missionary service, I felt I had come home.

I certify that a knowledge of the sealing power of the priesthood can bless us now as well as in the eternities. That knowledge became an anchor to an unsettled and drifting boy many years ago.

# 9

## BECOMING LIKE OUR FATHER IN HEAVEN

*Through the sealing powers of the holy priesthood,*
*all who participate in temple worship (on both sides of the*
*veil) have the promise that they may become*
*like our Father in Heaven.*

The doctrine of deification—that we may become like God and heirs of *all* things that our Heavenly Parents possess—is perhaps the greatest, most powerful, bold, and sacred doctrine associated with the restoration of all things in this dispensation of the fulness of times. It is a doctrine that must be reverenced and protected. To think that we may become possessors of the same powers and blessings as Deity, the supreme Beings of the universe, is incomprehensible in its totality to our finite minds. But that is exactly what the promises, associated with the sealing ordinance of eternal marriage, tell us. Here are the Lord's words:

> And again, verily I say unto you, if a man marry a
> wife by my word, which is my law, and by the new and

everlasting covenant, and it is sealed unto them by the Holy Spirit of promise, by him who is anointed, unto whom I have appointed this power and the keys of this priesthood . . . it shall be done unto them in all things whatsoever my servant hath put upon them, in time, and through all eternity; and shall be of full force when they are out of the world; and they shall pass by the angels, and the gods, which are set there, to their exaltation and glory in all things, as hath been sealed upon their heads, which glory shall be a fulness and a continuation of the seeds forever and ever.

Then shall they be gods, because they have no end; therefore shall they be from everlasting to everlasting, because they continue; then shall they be above all, because all things are subject unto them. Then shall they be gods, because they have all power, and the angels are subject unto them. (D&C 132:19–20)

Through the inspired explanation of prophets, we know that none of us will obtain exaltation singly, by ourselves. As we learn in the temple, exaltation is a corporate enterprise involving a man, a woman, and the Lord:

If you want salvation in the fullest, that is exaltation in the kingdom of God, so that you may become his sons and his daughters, you have got to go into the temple of the Lord and receive these holy ordinances which belong to that house, which cannot be had elsewhere. No man shall receive the fulness of eternity, of exaltation, alone; no woman shall receive that blessing alone; but man and wife, when they receive the sealing power in the temple of the Lord, if they thereafter keep all the commandments, shall pass on to exaltation, and shall continue and become like the Lord. And that is the destiny of men; that is what the Lord desires for his children.[1]

I love those words. To become gods is the destiny of the exalted: "All things are theirs" (D&C 76:59). President Joseph Fielding Smith, tenth president of the Church, pulled no punches in his description of exaltation. In what is perhaps the boldest, clearest, and most succinct statement of the ramifications of this doctrine, he said:

> The Father has promised us that through our faithfulness we shall be blessed with the fulness of his kingdom. In other words we will have the privilege of becoming like him. To become like him we must have all the powers of godhood; thus a man and his wife when glorified will have spirit children who eventually will go on an earth like this one we are on and pass through the same kind of experiences, being subject to mortal conditions, and if faithful, then they also will receive the fulness of exaltation and partake of the same blessings. There is no end to this development; it will go on forever. We will become gods. . . . We will have an endless eternity for this.[2]

This sacred promise of the Father to us is made by "an oath and covenant that cannot be broken."[3] We ought to treat this promise with great reverence.

The implications of President Smith's comments are significant, for they teach us not only that we may become as God is, but also that we have eternity to accomplish this goal. This is, in fact, what the Prophet Joseph Smith taught toward the end of his mortal ministry:

> Here, then, is eternal life—to know the only wise and true God; and you have got to learn how to be Gods

yourselves, and to be kings and priests to God, the same as all Gods have done before you, namely, by going from one small degree to another, and from a small capacity to a great one; from grace to grace, from exaltation to exaltation, until you attain to the resurrection of the dead, and are able to dwell in everlasting burnings, and to sit in glory, as do those who sit enthroned in everlasting power. And I want you to know that God, in the last days, while certain individuals are proclaiming his name, is not trifling with you or me.[4]

This is a challenging doctrine to some, as the Prophet acknowledged.[5] But he did not back away from it. On June 16, 1844, just days before his martyrdom, in the grove of trees east of the Nauvoo Temple, the Prophet Joseph offered a clarification to the King James text of Revelation 1:6, which reads: "And [Jesus Christ] hath made us kings and priests unto God and his Father: to him be glory and domin- ion for ever and ever. Amen." In June 1844, Joseph wanted to make known the whole truth about God and the Saints' opportunity to become like him. He said of this King James text:

It is altogether correct in the translation. Now, you know that of late some malicious and corrupt men have sprung up and apostatized from the Church of Jesus Christ of Latter- day Saints, and they declare that the Prophet believes in a plurality of Gods. . . . It reads just so in the [book of] Revelation, hence the doctrine of a plurality of Gods is as prominent in the Bible as any other doctrine. . . . Paul says there are Gods many and Lords many. . . . If Jesus Christ was the Son of God, and John discovered that God the Father of Jesus Christ had a Father, you may suppose that He had a

Father also. Where was there ever a son without a father?
And where was there ever a father without first being a son?[6]

Joseph Smith taught the truth and was condemned by some for it. But the truth could not be destroyed with him. Because of him we know that we are following a grand pattern as we strive to lay hold on the blessings of God and progress to become like him. Others before us followed this pattern. This is what is meant, in part, by the scriptural phrase, God's "course is one eternal round" (D&C 3:2; 35:1; see 1 Nephi 10:19; Alma 7:20).

Many other apostles and prophets have confirmed the validity of both the plurality of gods and the great promise that man may become as God is. Perhaps the affirmation of this doctrine most often quoted is the couplet of Lorenzo Snow, fifth president of the Church:

> As man now is, God once was;
> As God now is, man may be.[7]

President Snow indicated that this insight was revealed to him by inspiration. And though Latter-day Saints have been criticized and even accused of blasphemy for believing such things, the whole notion of deification (Greek, *theosis*) has a very long history that takes us back to the Old Testament. Moses, for example, was made "a god [*'elohim*] to Pharaoh" (Exodus 7:1). Later, the psalmist wrote, "I have said, Ye are gods [*'elohim*]" (Psalm 82:6). It is reported by John that Jesus quoted this very passage to a group of Jews about to stone him (John 10:34). In fact, it has been argued by some non-LDS scholars that "the Johannine corpus is an especially rich witness to theosis (John 3:8; 14:21–23;

15:4–8; 17:21–23; 1 John 3:2; 4:12). Commenting on 'John the Theologian' and his many references to our union with God, Peter of Damascus invokes the authority of Christ himself: we become 'gods by adoption through grace,' and, having become dispassionate, 'we have God within ourselves—as Christ Himself has told us.'"[8]

Another New Testament text indicating that the primitive Church enjoyed a rich understanding of man's destiny to become like God comes from 2 Peter 1:4: "Whereby are given unto us exceeding great and marvelous promises: that by these ye might be partakers of the divine nature."

We do not find this rich understanding of the doctrine of deification to have been lost once we leave the New Testament. Rather, it is "echoed by the fathers and the theologians of every age,"[9] especially the postapostolic writers. Irenaeus, a second-century theologian and premier churchman of his day, parallels Lorenzo Snow in his witness: "If the Word is made man, it is that men might become gods."[10] Also in the second century, Clement of Alexandria wrote: "Yea, I say, the Word of God became a man so that you might learn from a man how to become a god,"[11] which again is a parallel to President Snow's couplet. And finally, the second-century apologist Justin Martyr stated that men "were made like God, free from suffering and death . . . deemed worthy of becoming gods and of having power to become sons of the highest."[12]

These prominent writers lived within a hundred years of the original apostles and likely could trace their foundational beliefs to the foundational witnesses themselves. In other words, the doctrine of deification was not a radical or fringe belief. It was part of the core of early Christian conviction.

The doctrine of becoming like God did not die out after the second century, nor was it ignored. In fact, it was given powerful support, as we see in two of the most famous early medieval theologians of the Roman Catholic Church: Athanasius (for whom the Athanasian Creed is named) and the incomparable Augustine.

The former gave to the world what has become known as the Athanasian epigram, anticipating Lorenzo Snow by fifteen hundred years: "God became man so that men might become gods."[13] Athanasius expounded on his aphorism: "The Word was made flesh in order that we might be enabled to be made gods. . . . Just as the Lord, putting on the body, became a man, so also we men are both deified through his flesh, and henceforth inherit everlasting life."[14]

Augustine is credited with being one of the most influential thinkers in western civilization, perhaps one of the two or three greatest theologians in the history of Christian thought. He articulates the doctrine of deification as though he had been coached by Latter-day Saints: "But he himself that justifies also deifies, for by justifying he makes sons of God. 'For he has given them power to become the sons of God' [John 1:12]. If then we have been made sons of God, we have also been made gods."[15]

Many other witnesses could be cited to affirm the antiquity and centrality of the doctrine of becoming like God— becoming gods through the gospel of Jesus Christ. Eastern Orthodox Christianity has embraced the doctrine since its official establishment in A.D. 1054. In modern times, honest theologians have not been able to ignore the biblically based tenet that God has always intended to make his children heirs of all that he possesses (Romans 8:14–18; Galatians 4:7).

One of the most famous non-LDS commentators on the doctrine of deification in recent memory has been C. S. Lewis, Anglican churchman and Oxford don. He was a profound Christian thinker and prolific writer who considered deeply the ramifications of God's promises in the Bible: "It is a serious thing to live in a society of possible gods and goddesses, to remember that the dullest and most uninteresting person you can talk to may one day be a creature which, if you saw it now, you would be strongly tempted to worship."[16]

Professor Lewis strongly believed that Jesus Christ came into the world to help each of us become a son or daughter of God and also "a little Christ."[17] Thus, in words that closely parallel those of President Snow as well as those of early church Fathers, Lewis said: "The Son of God became a man to enable man to become sons of God."[18] Then, in what is perhaps his most complete statement about humans becoming gods, Lewis describes what the biblical injunction to "be perfect" really means:

> The command Be ye perfect is not idealistic gas. Nor is it a command to do the impossible. He is going to make us into creatures that can obey that command. He said (in the Bible) that we were "gods" and He is going to make good His words. If we let Him—for we can prevent Him, if we choose—He will make the feeblest and filthiest of us into a god or goddess, a dazzling, radiant, immortal creature, pulsating all through with such energy and joy and wisdom and

love as we cannot now imagine, a bright stainless mirror which reflects back to God perfectly (though, of course, on a smaller scale) His own boundless power and delight and goodness. The process will be long and in parts very painful; but that is what we are in for. Nothing less. He meant what He said.[19]

Perhaps our Father in Heaven's *greatest* power is his ability to elevate his children to the status and kind of life he himself enjoys. His power becomes our power, but it comes to us only through the atonement of Jesus Christ and the sealing ordinances of the priesthood administered in dedicated temples of the Lord. God does indeed mean what he said, as C. S. Lewis declared, but it can only happen in temples of the Lord. No wonder temples must be kept sacred. Nothing less would do as repositories of the ultimate gift and greatest power in the universe—where godhood is taught to sons and daughters of Heavenly Parents and bestowed upon them. Once we have been to the temple, we, like the ancients, confess that we are clearly strangers and pilgrims on the earth, awaiting arrival at the promised destination (Hebrews 11:13).

# 10

## ESTABLISHING AND NURTURING ETERNAL FAMILIES

*The purpose for which temples are constructed is also
the same purpose for which this earth was created—
establishing and nurturing eternal families.*

In a significant if sometimes overlooked revelation given in
the spring of 1831, the Lord decreed the purpose for which
this earth was created: "And again, verily I say unto you, that
whoso forbiddeth to marry is not ordained of God, for marriage is ordained of God unto man. Wherefore, it is lawful
that he should have one wife, and they twain shall be one
flesh, and all this that the earth might answer the end of its
creation; and that it might be filled with the measure of man,
according to his creation before the world was made" (D&C
49:15–17).

The Lord does not trifle with us nor take lightly the
importance of marriage and family life. This earth was made
for the express purpose of fostering these relationships. So
important is the link between the creation of the earth and

everlasting family bonds that the Lord himself testified that if the hearts of children and parents are not turned toward each other and welded together through the priesthood, the whole earth—its creation and maintenance—would be wasted at the Savior's second coming: "Behold, I will reveal unto you the Priesthood, by the hand of Elijah the prophet, before the coming of the great and dreadful day of the Lord. And he shall plant in the hearts of the children the promises made to the fathers, and the hearts of the children shall turn to their fathers. If it were not so, the whole earth would be utterly wasted at his coming" (D&C 2:1–3).

It cannot be stated too strongly. Without eternal families, this earth would be wasted. This doctrine is so significant that the foregoing passage constitutes one of only a small handful of passages that appear nearly verbatim in all the standard works. These passages in part, form the doctrinal basis for our priorities in life. We ought to do everything in our power to ensure a rich, vibrant, love-filled family life. Furthermore, in light of this doctrine of eternal families, we see how Elder Boyd K. Packer's statement applies to us today more than ever: "The study of the doctrines of the gospel will improve behavior quicker than a study of behavior will improve behavior."[1] When it comes to understanding the purpose of this earth and the importance of the family in the Father's plan for us, the counsel and example of the world as a whole are too skewed and corrupt to be of any help to us.

In a worldwide training broadcast to Church leaders in 2004, President James E. Faust recounted the sorry state of the world relative to family life. He said society in recent times has been plagued with a cancer: the "disintegration of many of our homes and families." He noted that this cancer "engulfs us." A reluctance to commit to marriage is dramatically increasing worldwide. Divorce rates are up, and "out-of-wedlock births have increased by 158 percent. . . . Another disturbing challenge to the family is that children are becoming less valued. In many parts of the world, people are having fewer children. Abortion is probably the clearest sign that couples do not want children. An estimated one-quarter of all pregnancies worldwide end by induced abortion. The rates range from a high of almost 50 percent in Europe to about 15 percent in Africa."[2]

President Gordon B. Hinckley went a step further: "No one need tell you that we are living in a very difficult season in the history of the world. Standards are dropping everywhere. Nothing seems to be sacred any more. . . . The family appears to be falling apart. The traditional family is under heavy attack. I do not know that things were worse in the times of Sodom and Gomorrah. . . . Notwithstanding [Abraham's] pleas, things were so bad that Jehovah decreed their destruction. They and their wicked inhabitants were annihilated. We see similar conditions today. They prevail all across the world. I think our Father must weep as He looks down upon His wayward sons and daughters."[3]

Our only hope, our only rescue, our only antidote to the poison and downward spiral of the world is in the sure word of the Lord and in the sealing power of the priesthood found in the Lord's temples. The Prophet Joseph Smith knew the problem and taught the solution: "How shall God come to the rescue of this generation? He will send Elijah the prophet. . . . Elijah shall reveal the covenants to seal the hearts of the fathers to the children, and the children to the fathers. . . . The Melchizedek Priesthood holds the right from the eternal God, and not by descent from father and mother; and that priesthood is as eternal as God Himself, having neither beginning of days nor end of life."[4]

We go to the temples of the Lord to receive that which Elijah restored—the keys and powers of the everlasting priesthood. Temples are the only places on earth where the hearts of parents and children can be sealed together with an unbreakable bond. Inherent in the fulness of the authority of the Melchizedek Priesthood is the power to anoint us, to seal us, and to ensure that we will inherit eternal life, a promise that was issued by our Father in Heaven eons ago, and predicated wholly on our loyalty to him and his Son.

Only in the Lord's temples do we find rock-solid guarantees that our most cherished relationships can last forever and be healed of all hurts. The world cannot give us what we want. "In order for you to receive your children to yourselves you must have a promise—some ordinance; some blessing, in order to ascend above principalities," said Joseph Smith.[5] The temples of the Lord provide that promise and that ordinance. And the sealing ordinance has an effect on both this life and the next, on both time and eternity. It changes the way we look at earthly priorities, and it determines our possibilities for eternity. Participation in the sealing ordinance invites—in truth, motivates—us to cultivate and safeguard our true treasure, our families.

Wealth, power, or high position, whether in or out of the Church, does not insulate us from the world or give us lasting happiness or peace. Such things do not guarantee us eternal life nor help us attain the kind of existence our Father in Heaven enjoys. Only the sealing ordinances provided in the temple and the keys of the fulness of the priesthood restored by Elijah do that. The family unit, organized and sealed in the temple—not the social order of the gospel nor the holding of a particular office in the Church—is the basis of exaltation and the fulness of joy. To receive a fulness of joy, a man and a woman have to seek the blessings of the Lord like father Abraham did (Abraham 1:2) and receive all the rites and ordinances of the temple like the Lord himself. The Prophet Joseph Smith taught: "If a man gets a fulness of the priesthood of God he has to get it in the same way that Jesus Christ obtained it, and that was by keeping all the commandments and obeying all the ordinances of the house of the Lord."[6]

The Prophet Joseph also made plain the role of the sealing power in preparing the Lord's people for the second coming of Jesus Christ. He taught that this power has been restored in our day "to bring about the completion of the fullness of the Gospel, a fullness of the dispensation of dispensations, even the fullness of times . . . to prepare the earth for the return of His glory, even a celestial glory, and a kingdom of Priests and kings to God and the Lamb, forever, on Mount Zion, and with him the hundred and forty and four thousand whom John the Revelator saw, all of which is to come to pass in the restitution of all things."[7]

The ordinances of the temple administered in these last days have a direct and powerful role in establishing conditions that will allow the thousand-year era of peace to last. The Millennium will be ushered in by power

(Revelation 18:1–2; 19:11–16) and maintained by the righteousness of the people (1 Nephi 22:26).

The blessings and spiritual strength that derive from a society of families sealed together for eternity by priesthood power will be a principal factor in renewing the earth and preparing it to receive a paradisiacal state of glory in the Millennium.[8] Through the sealing power of the priesthood, the faithful, those who keep the covenants they have made in the temples and become priests and kings or priestesses and queens to God within the family of God, will reign with Christ in the Millennium and throughout eternity. Hence, the sealing power and the Millennium are inextricably connected.

It is by and through the sealing power of the priesthood, found in the Lord's holy temples and in no other place, that the purpose for which this earth was created will be fulfilled. It is also the means (and only the means) whereby men and women can enjoy the fulness of the celestial glory. In fact, if we refuse the sealing ordinances, our chances may not be so good for any portion of the celestial kingdom, even though we may have been baptized. Said the Prophet Joseph Smith: "Those who will not receive all the ordinances [of the temple] will come short of the fullness of that [celestial] glory, if they do not lose the whole."[9]

On the other hand, as prophets have also taught, not one of our Heavenly Father's sons or daughters will be denied any covenant, promise, or blessing if they desire it and have tried to remain worthy of it. No son or daughter who has not had the opportunity for marriage and family life in mortality for any number of legitimate reasons (early death, physical incapacity, lack of honorable marriage partner, etc.) will be denied those privileges in the eternities. This is one reason a glorious millennial era awaits us; to put things right.

The words of President Lorenzo Snow are of tremendous significance and comfort:

> *All will have an opportunity to marry.* A lady came into our office the other day and asked to see me on a private matter. She informed me that she felt very badly, because her opportunities for getting a husband had not been favorable. She was about thirty years of age, and she wanted to know what her condition would be in the other life, if she did not succeed in getting a husband in this life. I suppose this question arises in the hearts of our young people, especially the marriageable sisters and the young widows; and some very foolish doctrine has been presented to some of the sisters in regard to this and other things of a kindred nature. I desire to give a little explanation for the comfort and consolation of parties in this condition. There is no Latter-day Saint who dies after having lived a faithful life who will lose anything because of having failed to do certain things when opportunities were not furnished him or her. In other words, if a young man or a young woman has no opportunity of getting married, and they live faithful lives up to the time of their death, they will have all the blessings, exaltation, and glory that any man or woman will have who had this opportunity and improved it. That is sure and positive.[10]

Marriage is an act of faith. Those who have the appropriate opportunity in mortality to marry ought to act upon it. Those who do not must have faith that it will happen some day. Earth, family, temple, sealing power, and celestial glory all go together. They are inseparably connected. Ultimately and eternally, this earth will become the everlasting abode of those who have been sealed together as families. "Therefore, it must needs be sanctified from all unrighteousness, that it may be prepared for the celestial glory; for after it hath filled the measure of its creation, it shall be crowned with glory, even with the presence of God the Father; that bodies who are of the celestial kingdom may possess it forever and ever; for, for this intent was it made and created, and for this intent are they sanctified" (D&C 88:18–20).

The eternal purposes and plans of God cannot, will not, be thwarted. The ultimate destiny of the earth will not be changed. Family life will not be destroyed. The Church will not fail. All these will be protected and preserved by the sealing power of the eternal priesthood administered in temples. The Lord's temples will see us through the storms and tight places of mortality. The sealing ordinances and covenants of the temple will preserve our families beyond the grave and, through the atonement of Christ, give to each of us the power and knowledge to rise in the resurrection with bodies capable of continuing marriage and family relationships. But it needs to be said that marriage and family life will continue for eternity only in the celestial kingdom and by participating in the ordinances established for those purposes: "Except a man and his wife enter into an everlasting covenant and be married for eternity, while in this probation, by the power and authority of the Holy Priesthood, they will cease to increase when they die; that is, they will not have any children after the resurrection. But those who are married by the power and authority of the priesthood . . . will continue to increase and have children in the celestial glory."[11] By the very nature of what happens inside, temples testify that every blessing of God is available to every one of his children in eternity.

Our happiness in the life to come will be eternal because the family continues. President Joseph Fielding Smith was an articulate teacher on the eternal nature of families. He said: "Not only was marriage instituted by the Lord to endure eternally, but it also naturally follows that the same is true of the family. . . . Is it possible to imagine a greater source of sorrow than to be left in the eternal world without claim on father or mother or children?"[12] He went on to state that a situation in which no family ties bind individuals together, where no natural affection exists, is a circumstance "of horror." Could there ever be any happiness this way? Could it ever be heaven? No, the

> family is the unit in the kingdom of God. . . . We believe that the family will go on. I get a great deal of comfort out of the thought that if I am faithful and worthy of an exaltation, my father will be my father, and I will be subject to him as his son through all eternity; that I will recognize and know my mother and she will be my mother in all eternity; and my brothers and sisters will be my brothers and sisters for all eternity; and that my children and my wives will be mine in eternity. I don't know how some other people feel, but that is a glorious thought to me.[13]

So it is for all of us. God be thanked for the creation of this earth and the priesthood sealing power found in temples that allows the earth to fulfill the measure of its creation. Temples illuminate the way of eternal happiness for each of us and seal us not only to each other but to our Heavenly Parents, the perfect nurturers. Marriage for time and eternity fulfills the crowning achievement of our Father in Heaven, making us heirs of *all* he possesses.

# 11

## ADAM AND EVE RECEIVED
## THE SEALING ORDINANCES

*The fulness of the gospel of Jesus Christ, including the
sealing ordinances performed in our temples today, was
revealed to the first mortals on earth, Adam and Eve,
who stand at the head of the human family.*

This earth was created and our first parents, Adam and Eve,
placed upon it with physical bodies only *after* the plan of
salvation and its ordinances were established and made known
to all of our Father's spirit children. These ordinances were
"instituted in the heavens before the foundation of the world,
in the priesthood, for the salvation of men" and "are not to be
altered or changed,"[1] although the manner of presentation has
varied over time. The Prophet Joseph Smith further stated
that "all that were ever saved, were saved through the power
of this great plan of redemption, as much before the coming
of Christ as since; if not, God has had different plans in operation (if we may so express it), to bring men back to dwell with
Himself; and this we cannot believe."[2]

Thus, Adam, Eve, and all their posterity will be saved by

adherence to the same gospel principles.[3] Adam and Eve were required to participate in the sealing ordinances, just as you and I are. This is all the more impressive when we consider Adam's and Eve's premortal status, which tells us much about their greatness.

From the temple as well as from scripture, we learn that Adam was Michael the Archangel, one of the "noble and great ones" in our premortal existence (Abraham 3:22), who led the righteous in the war in heaven against the adversary and his hosts (Revelation 12:7–9). He

> attained a stature and power second only to that of Christ, the Firstborn. None of all the billions of our Father's children equalled him in intelligence and might, save Jesus only. He sat in the council of the gods in the planning of the creation of this earth, and then, under Christ, participated in the creative enterprise. (Abra. 3:22–26.) He was foreordained to come to earth as the father of the human race, and when Lucifer and one-third of the hosts of heaven rebelled, Adam (with the exalted title of Michael the Archangel) led the hosts of the righteous in the war in heaven. (Rev. 12:7–9.)[4]

Though we know less about Eve, "without question she was like unto her mighty husband, Adam, in intelligence and in devotion to righteousness."[5]

When Adam and Eve were placed in the garden of Eden, however, they experienced the great equalizer that affects all mortals—the veil of forgetfulness. It caused them to become as little children, not remembering their premortal status, and required them to be taught and to walk by faith. The education of Adam and Eve progressed under the tutelage of God and angels. These divine messengers modeled for us a perfect pedagogy, or method of teaching. They first taught the plan of redemption and then enumerated the specific commandments. In other words, doctrines and principles preceded specific do's and don'ts (a pedagogy also followed in the temple):

> And after God had appointed that these things should come unto man, behold, then he saw that it was expedient that man should know concerning the things whereof he had appointed unto them;
>
> Therefore he sent angels to converse with them, who caused men to behold of his glory. . . .
>
> Therefore God gave unto them commandments, after having made known unto them the plan of redemption, that they should not do evil, the penalty thereof being a second death, which was an everlasting death as to things pertaining unto righteousness; for on such the plan of redemption could have no power, for the works of justice could not be destroyed, according to the supreme goodness of God. (Alma 12:28–29, 32)

President Ezra Taft Benson was clear that the same teachings and requirements of exaltation we receive in our day were the same concepts given to our first parents:

> When our Heavenly Father placed Adam and Eve on this earth, He did so with the purpose in mind of teaching them how to regain His presence. Our Father promised a Savior to redeem them from their fallen condition. He gave to them the plan of salvation and told them to teach their children faith in Jesus Christ and repentance. Further, Adam and his posterity were commanded by God to be baptized, to receive the Holy Ghost, and to enter into the order of the Son of God.

To enter into the order of the Son of God is the equivalent today of entering into the fullness of the Melchizedek
Priesthood, which is only received in the house of the Lord.

Because Adam and Eve had complied with these
requirements, God said to them, "Thou art after the order of
him who was without beginning of days or end of years, from
all eternity to all eternity." (Moses 6:67.)[6]

Many prophets from the beginning of time onward have
taught that Adam and Eve received the fulness of the gospel
of Jesus Christ. Moses 5:58–59 are foundational verses: "And
thus the Gospel began to be preached, from the beginning,
being declared by holy angels sent forth from the presence of
God, and by his own voice, and by the gift of the Holy
Ghost. And thus all things were confirmed unto Adam, by
an holy ordinance, and the Gospel preached, and a decree
sent forth, that it should be in the world, until the end
thereof; and thus it was. Amen."

Though we are not told specifically in scripture the
nature of the "holy ordinance" by which all things were confirmed unto Adam and Eve, we can imagine. Adam and Eve
participated in the sealing ordinances and marriage covenant
and so became eternal companions through God's own
power. Joseph Smith taught that "marriage was an institution
of heaven, instituted in the Garden of Eden; [and] that it is
necessary it should be solemnized by the authority of the
everlasting priesthood."[7] To Adam was given Eve, a helper
"meet" for him, that is, perfectly suited, worthy, precisely
appropriate for him (which is the intended English meaning
behind the Hebrew phrase 'ezer k°negdo—of Genesis 2:18).
Or, in the words of President Joseph Fielding Smith, "a help

who would answer all the requirements, not only of companionship, but also through whom the fulness of the purposes of the Lord could be accomplished regarding the mission of man through mortal life and into eternity."[8] Therefore, the union of both Adam and Eve "was required to complete man in the image of God."[9]

A significant implication of President Smith's comment is that we have both a Heavenly Father and a Heavenly Mother, a truth borne out by scripture: "And God said, Let us make man in our own image, after our likeness. . . . So God created man in his own image, in the image of God created he him; male and female created he them" (Genesis 1:26–27). It is instructive to note that in the creation account in the book of Abraham, it is the "Gods," plural, who are responsible for creating man and woman (see Abraham 5:7–20). Thus, the Gods are of both genders, male and female.

Perhaps the biblical text uses the singular construction when referring to Deity because of the complete unity that exists between eternal marriage partners, specifically the Gods. Adam's response to receiving a companion perfectly suited to him reflects this oneness: "This [woman] is now bone of my bones, and flesh of my flesh" (Genesis 2:23). The Savior himself confirmed the doctrine of oneness in celestial marriage: "And he answered and said unto them, Have ye not read, that he which made them at the beginning made them male and female, and said, For this cause shall a man leave father and mother, and shall cleave to his wife: and they twain shall be one flesh? Wherefore they are no more twain, but one flesh. What therefore God hath joined together, let not man put asunder" (Matthew 19:4–6).

Possessing an understanding of the eternal ordinances and covenants of the plan of exaltation, Adam and Eve were sealed as husband and wife in the Garden of Eden before the Fall occurred. On this point, President Joseph Fielding Smith was clear:

> God the Father married Adam and Eve. Marriage as established in the beginning was an eternal covenant. The first man and the first woman were not married until death should part them, for at that time death had not come into the world. The ceremony on that occasion was performed by the Eternal Father himself whose work endures forever. It is the will of the Lord that all marriages should be of like character, and in becoming "one flesh" the man and the woman are to continue in the married status, according to the Lord's plan, throughout all eternity as well as in this mortal life.[10]

That which happens in temples today reflects the perfect pattern of heaven as well as that which happened from the beginning of time on this earth. As eternal marriage companions, sealed by God's own power, with their posterity (you and me) sealed to them in an everlasting bond, Adam and Eve have taken their place at the head of the human family. President Smith offered a succinct summary of our first parents' position and described the pattern that we too follow:

> Every married man stands at the head of his household, that is, his immediate family. Thus I, for instance, will stand at the head of my family group by virtue of the sealing for time and eternity, and my children will belong to me. I will belong to my parents in their family group. My father likewise, with his brothers and sisters, will belong to his father's unit in that family group, and his father to his father before

him—all linked together generation to generation like a chain. So it will be of the righteous from the days of Adam down—Adam standing at the head as Michael, having authority and jurisdiction over his posterity in this large family group who have kept the commandments of God.

Now that is the order of the priesthood. Of course there will be chains that will be broken, links that will be missing, because we can not force people into the kingdom. Those who are unworthy to be joined in this grouping of families will have to stand aside, and those who are worthy will be brought together and the chain will go on just the same.

Eventually, when this work is perfected, and Christ delivers up to his Father the keys and makes his report, and death is destroyed, then that great family from the days of Adam down, of all the righteous, those who have kept the commandments of God, will find that they are one family, the family of God, entitled to all the blessings that pertain to the exaltation.[11]

How much we owe to the sealing power of the priesthood. All who receive the associated ordinances and live worthy of their temple covenants will enjoy the ultimate blessings of the sealing power. They will become exalted beings, heirs of God, and participants with the Gods in eternal family relationships. I am sobered and humbled to think (and it is no exaggeration to say) that not only am I sealed to kings and queens, gods and goddesses, but I was born to be a king, to become royalty in the eternities—and so were you. All those who gain exaltation in the celestial kingdom "receive the fullness of the power, might, and dominion of that kingdom. They overcome all things. They are crowned as priests and kings [priestesses and queens] and become like [God]."[12] That is the essence of everything we learn in the Lord's temples.

# 12

## TEMPLE ORDINANCES IN EARLIER DISPENSATIONS

*Many righteous people, from the time of Adam through*
*the days of the early Christian apostles, received the same*
*ordinances of exaltation as did our first parents,*
*the same ordinances available today.*

Several sources indicate that many individuals from Adam to Abraham participated in what we today call temple ordinances. The official explanation of Facsimile 2 from the book of Abraham teaches this truth:

> Fig. 3. Is made to represent God, sitting upon his throne, clothed with power and authority; with a crown of eternal light upon his head; representing also the grand Key-words of the Holy Priesthood, as revealed to Adam in the Garden of Eden, as also to Seth, Noah, Melchizedek, Abraham, and all to whom the Priesthood was revealed.
>
> Fig. 7. Represents God sitting upon his throne, revealing through the heavens the grand Key-words of the Priesthood; as, also, the sign of the Holy Ghost unto Abraham, in the form of a dove.

Fig. 8. Contains writings that cannot be revealed unto the world; but is to be had in the Holy Temple of God.

Some of these individuals in ancient times were so faithful to their covenants that they were translated, physically removed from this earth without tasting death for a time. From the Joseph Smith Translation of Genesis 14 we learn of these remarkable disciples, the archetypal one being Enoch:

Now Melchizedek was a man of faith, who wrought righteousness; and when a child he feared God, and stopped the mouths of lions, and quenched the violence of fire.

And thus, having been approved of God, he was ordained an high priest after the order of the covenant which God made with Enoch . . .

For God having sworn unto Enoch and unto his seed with an oath by himself; that every one being ordained after this order and calling should have power, by faith, to break mountains, to divide the seas, to dry up waters, to turn them out of their course;

To put at defiance the armies of nations, to divide the earth, to break every band, to stand in the presence of God; to do all things according to his will, according to his command, subdue principalities and powers; and this by the will of the Son of God which was from before the foundation of the world.

And men having this faith, coming up unto this order of God, were translated and taken up into heaven.

And now, Melchizedek was a priest of this order; therefore he obtained peace in Salem, and was called the Prince of peace.

And his people wrought righteousness, and obtained heaven, and sought for the city of Enoch which God had before taken, separating it from the earth, having reserved it unto the latter days, or the end of the world. (JST Genesis 14:26–27, 30–34)

These verses disclose the spiritual standard required of those who were worthy to be translated. They exercised mighty faith, participated in all priesthood ordinances, were redeemed from their fallen state, became reconciled to God (were at one with him), gained an assurance of celestial glory, and felt secure enough with the things of righteousness that they actively sought for the presence of heaven.

In other words, certain ancient patriarchs and prophets received and honored the covenants and ordinances of the fulness of the priesthood to such an extent that they could no longer be held on the earth. Most of them are unnamed: "And men having this faith, coming up unto this order of God, were translated and taken up into heaven" (JST Genesis 14:32). We know the people of the city of Enoch were among them (Moses 7:21), as were the people of Melchizedek (JST Genesis 14:34). In fact, Alma implies that it was the ordinances of salvation administered through the priesthood of Melchizedek that enabled the people to repent (they were among the worst sinners) and obtain a state of profound righteousness such as that enjoyed by Enoch and his translated people (Alma 13:13–19; especially v. 16; JST Genesis 14:34–36). As a result of Melchizedek's saving work, the higher priesthood was renamed in his honor (D&C 107:2–4), and he became a type and foreshadowing of Christ (Alma 13:18).

The Prophet Joseph Smith enlarged our understanding of the nature, ministries, and location of translated beings:

Now the doctrine of translation is a power which belongs to this Priesthood. There are many things which belong to the powers of the Priesthood and the keys thereof, that have been kept hid from before the foundation of the world; they are hid from the wise and prudent to be revealed in the last times.

Many have supposed that the doctrine of translation was a doctrine whereby men were taken immediately into the presence of God, and into an eternal fullness, but this is a mistaken idea. Their place of habitation is that of the terrestrial order, and a place prepared for such characters He held in reserve to be ministering angels unto many planets, and who as yet have not entered into so great a fullness as those who are resurrected from the dead.[1]

Probably the most recognized of our forefathers who participated in all the ordinances of the temple for the living—washings, anointings, and sealings—are Abraham, Isaac, and Jacob. In the same section of the Doctrine and Covenants that describes the nature of the sealing ordinance of eternal marriage and the promises associated with it, these great patriarchs are commended by the Lord "because they did none other things than that which they were commanded; and because they did none other things than that which they were commanded, they have entered into their exaltation, according to the promises, and sit upon thrones, and are not angels but are gods" (D&C 132:37).

The ancient patriarchs had the same covenants, ordinances, promises, and blessings that we have today in our temples. Elder Marion G. Romney stated: "Temples are to us all what Bethel was to Jacob."[2] Elder Bruce R. McConkie taught that we who live in this present marvelous dispensation really have nothing over the ancients, for they enjoyed an unsurpassed knowledge of the Lord's mysteries:

We are in process of receiving all that God has spoken by the mouths of all his holy prophets since the world began. Only a small portion has come to us so far; we do not, as yet, begin to know what the ancients knew. . . .

Except for a few things relative to salvation for the dead, we have not yet received one syllable of scripture, one trace of truth, one gospel verity, one saving power, that was not had anciently.

The time is yet future—it will be Millennial—when the Lord reveals to us those things which have been hidden from the foundation of the earth and which have never as yet been given to man. . . .

What we have so far received is to test our faith. When we repent of all our iniquity and become clean before the Lord, and when we exercise faith in him like unto the brother of Jared, then the sealed portion of the ancient word will be translated and read from the housetops.[3]

We know of specific prophets living in the period between Abraham and Jesus Christ who enjoyed the ordinances of exaltation, exercised the keys of the priesthood, controlled the elements, and displayed dramatic power: Moses, Nathan, Elijah, and Alma. All the prophets held the Melchizedek Priesthood and were ordained by God himself, according to Joseph Smith.[4] But Moses, Elijah, and Alma were also translated.[5] They joined the ranks of Enoch, Melchizedek, and their peoples. In the case of Moses and Elijah, we know they returned to earth to pass on their keys of power and knowledge (see Matthew 17:1–3; D&C 110:11–16). And we believe Alma and others have returned as well. The Prophet Joseph Smith listed some of those who have returned, including "divers angels, from Michael or Adam down to the present time, all declaring their dispensation, their keys, their honors, their majesty and glory, and the power of their priesthood" (D&C 128:20–21). Evidence indicates that Joseph Smith received special revelation on the doctrine of translated beings, including a visitation from Enoch.[6]

During the period that witnessed the rise and tragic fall of King David, the prophet Nathan as well as other prophets held the sealing keys, as modern revelation attests: "David's wives and concubines were given unto him of me [the Lord], by the hand of Nathan, my servant, and others of the prophets who had the keys of this power" (D&C 132:39).

In the meridian dispensation, the ordinances of exaltation were made available. President Heber C. Kimball taught that the temple endowment that operates in the Church in this dispensation operated in the ancient Church (first century after Christ). Furthermore, he said that Jesus "was the one that inducted his Apostles into these ordinances."[7] Closer to our day, President Joseph Fielding Smith and Elder Bruce R. McConkie stated that it was their belief that Peter, James, and John received the endowment on the Mount of Transfiguration. Because they were instructed not to tell of the occurrences on the Mount until after Jesus was "risen . . . from the dead" (Matthew 17:9), it appears that similar blessings may not have been given to other members of the Twelve or to the Church until after the Savior's resurrection.[8]

The New Testament teaches that during his forty-day postresurrection ministry, Jesus spent time specifically with the apostles, "to whom also he shewed himself alive after his passion by many infallible proofs . . . and speaking of the things pertaining to the kingdom of God" (Acts 1:3).

The phrase "infallible proofs" is the King James translation of the Greek word *tekmeriois* and means, literally, "sure signs or tokens." The book of Acts is really saying that Jesus taught the apostles about his resurrection and about the kingdom of God through many sure signs or tokens. It is the same in the Lord's temples today.

The Prophet Joseph Smith said that Jesus taught the Jews the concepts of baptism for the dead as well as washings and anointings. Furthermore, he said that the chief apostle, Peter, performed washings, anointings, etc., on the Day of Pentecost in a house "God obtained." We would like to know what Joseph meant by "etcetera," but he did not elaborate.[9] Neither did he discuss the house "God obtained." But we do recognize a pattern of temple ordinances being performed across dispensations.

There are strong suggestions and clues from apocryphal texts and early Christian histories that temple teachings and rituals or practices were well known by many of the early disciples of the Lord. For example, in his famous work *Ecclesiastical History*, the renowned early church historian Eusebius (A.D. 260–340) wrote, "After the resurrection the Lord imparted the higher knowledge to James the Just, John, and Peter. They gave it to the other apostles, and the other apostles to the Seventy, one of whom was Barnabas."[10] Eusebius also referred to the teachings of Jesus as "the mysteries."[11]

In a later Christian text, a Coptic writing entitled 2 Jeu, "the Lord, after the resurrection, orders the apostles to clothe themselves in white linen robes, then orders them to be washed again; he seals them, after which they receive fire in the spirit at their spiritual baptism."[12] Another later Christian text from Oxyrhynchus in Egypt, dating from between the third and fifth centuries, is set in the court of the Jerusalem Temple. One of the high priests meets Jesus and takes him to task, saying, "What is this talk about being pure? I am pure. I am pure, for I have washed in the pool of David and I have changed my old clothes and put on the white garments; and being thus purified, I proceeded and participated in the holy ordinances and handled the holy vessels." Jesus replies to him, "The dogs and the pigs have bathed upstream from the pool of David where you bathed. You anointed yourself, but the whore and the tax collectors do that. They bathe and anoint themselves and put on fair garments, but does that cause them to be pure?"[13]

Professor Nibley makes a significant interpretive comment on this passage: "Jesus is not making fun of the purification and anointing, but is saying that the garment is inadequate without the thing that it signifies. It will not protect you unless you are true and faithful to your covenant, and only to the degree to which you do not dishonor your garment has it any significance at all."[14]

A final example comes from a document called the Apocalypse of Moses. Thought to have been composed by a Jewish writer in the third or fourth century after Christ, the text was almost certainly known by early Christian groups as well. It is an expanded version of early chapters of Genesis. Therein "Adam, after being washed three times in the Acherusian Lake, is conducted back to the third heaven [see Paul's comment in 2 Corinthians 12:2]. Then he is clothed in linen garments and anointed with oil, and prepared to go into the presence of the Father."[15]

These are remarkable examples when we think about it. They are solid evidence of a knowledge of endowment-like rituals in early Christian practice. But they should not surprise us. The temple was the center of society and community in the time of the biblical patriarchs, in ancient Israel, and in early Christianity.

With so many examples of the widespread knowledge of some or all of the ordinances of the holy temple—washings, anointings, clothing in holy garments, sealings, and preparations to enter God's presence—who can doubt the veracity of Elder David B. Haight's statement: "Saints of all ages have had temples in one form or another. There is evidence that temple worship was customary from Adam to Noah and that after the Flood the holy priesthood was continued; therefore, we have every reason to believe the ordinances of the temple were available to those entitled to receive them."[16]

It also seems clear that when apostasy overtook religious communities and destroyed the true authority to administer the holy ordinances of the endowment and attendant sealings, people looked to temple practices with longing and a sense that if they could demonstrate a knowledge of those sacred concepts, that would somehow legitimize their beliefs. Even those people who were reeling from the effects of apostasy recognized the purpose of the rituals: to redeem and bestow power to acquire eternal life. Without doubt, the covenants and ordinances we now enjoy through temple worship originate from a divine source. History teaches us that.

# 13

## GATHERING THE SAINTS FOR THE BUILDING OF TEMPLES

*The Lord's purpose in gathering the Saints in every dispensation has been for the building of temples in which to administer his ordinances.*

In June of 1843, a large assembly of Saints met at the temple in Nauvoo to hear the Prophet speak. They were eager to hear the Prophet's voice in the setting of the Lord's house. His message was clear. God gathers his people to build temples: "What was the object of gathering the Jews, or the people of God in any age of the world? . . . The main object was to build unto the Lord a house whereby He could reveal unto His people the ordinances of His house and the glories of His kingdom, and teach the people the way of salvation; for there are certain ordinances and principles that, when they are taught and practiced, must be done in a place or house built for that purpose."[1]

The Prophet indicated that sacred temples have always been a part of the Father's plan of exaltation for his children and were contemplated in our premortal existence: "It was the design of the councils of heaven before the world was, that the principles and laws of the priesthood should be predicated upon the gathering of the people in every age. . . . It is for the same purpose that God gathers together His people in the last days, to build unto the Lord a house to prepare them for the ordinances and endowments, washings and anointings, etc. One of the ordinances of the house of the Lord is baptism for the dead. God decreed *before the foundation of the world* that that ordinance should be administered in a font prepared for that purpose in the house of the Lord."[2]

Thus temples were foreordained and foreseen by God before we came to this earth. Perhaps we bring with us into mortality very faint memories, maybe even only wisps of thought, of our commitment to temples and temple worship made in premortality. Perhaps that is one of the reasons we feel we are returning home when we go to the temple. Lines from the poet William Wordsworth express the right sentiment:

> *Our birth is but a sleep and a forgetting:*
> *The Soul that rises with us, our life's Star,*
> *Hath had elsewhere its setting,*
> *And cometh from afar:*
> *Not in entire forgetfulness,*
> *And not in utter nakedness,*
> *But trailing clouds of glory do we come*
> *From God, who is our home.*[3]

We were acquainted with temples in our premortal heavenly home, and now they serve as a point of contact with everything that was good and right before we entered this fallen world.

By June 11, 1843, the date of Joseph Smith's discourse at the temple, the Prophet knew very well the importance of temples in the Lord's plan. The Nauvoo Temple where they stood represented the second successful effort by the Latter-day Saints to build and maintain a house of the Lord. Temple sites had been dedicated in Independence, Missouri; Kirtland, Ohio; Far West, Missouri; and Adam-ondi-Ahman, Missouri. Only the Kirtland Temple had been completed, but it was desecrated and lost to the Saints because of mob rule, as Brigham Young explained:

> The Saints had to flee before mobocracy. And, by toil and daily labor, they found places in Missouri, where they laid the corner stones of Temples, in Zion and her Stakes, and then had to retreat to Illinois, to save the lives of those who could get away alive from Missouri, where fell the Apostle David W. Patten, with many like associates, and where were imprisoned in loathsome dungeons, and fed on human flesh, Joseph and Hyrum, and many others. But before all this had transpired, the Temple at Kirtland had fallen into the hands of wicked men, and by them been polluted, like the Temple at Jerusalem, and consequently it was disowned by the Father and the Son.[4]

Thus, after so many setbacks, we detect in the revelation announcing the Lord's command to build yet another temple at Nauvoo (D&C 124:25–27) an outpouring of patience, affection, and understanding on the part of the Lord, as well as an extended explanation to Joseph and the Saints regarding the importance and eternal significance of temples. According to the plan of exaltation, another temple was now required, even though others had been lost to the enemy. The Lord said:

> For there is not a place found on earth that he may come to and restore again that which was lost unto you, or which he hath taken away, even the fulness of the priesthood. . . .

119

For therein are the keys of the holy priesthood ordained, that you may receive honor and glory. . . .

And again, verily I say unto you, how shall your washings be acceptable unto me, except ye perform them in a house which you have built to my name?

For, for this cause I commanded Moses that he should build a tabernacle, that they should bear it with them in the wilderness, and to build a house in the land of promise, that those ordinances might be revealed which had been hid from before the world was.

Therefore, verily I say unto you, that your anointings, and your washings, and your baptisms for the dead, and your solemn assemblies, and your memorials for your sacrifices by the sons of Levi, and for your oracles in your most holy places wherein you receive conversations, and your statutes and judgments, for the beginning of the revelations and foundation of Zion, and for the glory, honor, and endowment of all her municipals, are ordained by the ordinance of my holy house, which my people are always commanded to build unto my holy name.

And verily I say unto you, let this house be built unto my name, that I may reveal mine ordinances therein unto my people. (D&C 124:28, 34, 37–40)

We also sense that section 124 was given to bolster the battered and beleaguered Saints:

And this I make an example unto you, for your consolation concerning all those who have been commanded to do a work and have been hindered by the hands of their enemies, and by oppression, saith the Lord your God.

For I am the Lord your God, and will save all those of

your brethren who have been pure in heart, and have been slain in the land of Missouri, saith the Lord.

And again, verily I say unto you, I command you again to build a house to my name, even in this place, that you may prove yourselves unto me that ye are faithful in all things whatsoever I command you, that I may bless you, and crown you with honor, immortality, and eternal life. (D&C 124:53–55)

The Saints were driven from pillar to post, hounded by their enemies, and their best blood was sacrificed. But through it all the one constant was the Lord's command to build temples. I am deeply moved by the tremendous perseverance and resilience of the Saints in the face of hostility. They did as they were commanded and built more and more temples until now they dot the earth.

Though highlighted in Doctrine and Covenants 124, the tabernacle in Moses' day was probably not the first structure set apart as a house of the Lord for the purpose of administering priesthood ordinances. Adam and his righteous posterity down to the time of Noah may have built such structures; we have no concrete information. Some evidence exists, however, that indicates a temple was located on Mount Moriah during Melchizedek's life before he was translated and, thus, existed during Abraham's early life. The Jewish historian Josephus (A.D. 38–100) wrote that "[Melchizedek] the Righteous King, for such he really was; on which account he was [there] the first priest of God, and first built a temple, [there,] and called the city Jerusalem, which was formerly called Salem."[5] During the time Melchizedek was the Lord's presiding authority on the earth ("there were many before him, and also there were many afterwards, but none were greater"; Alma 13:19), he and Abraham lived not far from each other in Canaan. Early in his life Abraham had wanted to be a "prince of peace" (Abraham 1:2), as was Melchizedek.

Abraham prepared himself and received the priesthood from Melchizedek (see D&C 84:14), though we do not know when or where. Joseph Smith noted: "Abraham says to Melchizedek, I believe all that thou hast taught me *concerning the priesthood and the coming of the Son of Man;* so Melchizedek ordained Abraham and sent him away. Abraham rejoiced, saying, Now I have a priesthood."[6]

Possessing the Melchizedek Priesthood, Abraham could participate in every temple ordinance available to us living today, including the sealing ordinance, which he did (D&C 132:37). Perhaps he engaged in temple worship on Mount Moriah under Melchizedek's direction before he was commanded to go there with Isaac (Genesis 22:2). From Josephus's statement, we may conclude that Mount Moriah was already a place with holy associations when Abraham took Isaac there to be offered up, long before Solomon built his temple there. If Josephus's account is true, then Solomon's Temple was not the First Temple, even though that is its accepted designation. It was at the temple site on Mount Moriah, as well, where Jehovah appeared to Solomon's father, King David (2 Chronicles 3:1).

Past, present, and future continually come together at this sacred space. Mount Moriah was to be the place of centuries of sacrifices in anticipation of the Great Sacrifice that would be accomplished there by the earthly Messiah. That Moriah and the temple were to be memorialized as a place of peace above all else is confirmed in Jehovah's refusal to allow King

David to build the temple there because he was a man of war and had shed much blood, even though he was a man after the Lord's "own heart" (1 Samuel 13:14). He was permitted to collect materials for the temple's construction. But the construction and dedication were reserved for David's son Solomon (see 1 Kings 5:3; 2 Chronicles 6:7–9; 1 Chronicles 22:8). There is a great lesson here about the Lord's temples in general. They symbolize the Prince of Peace.

Between the time of Moses and the time of Jesus Christ, the house of Israel as a whole existed in a state of apostasy, which affected what was done in Solomon's and Herod's temples in Jerusalem. As we know, the ordinances practiced by the patriarchs from Adam to Moses were administered under the authority and power of the Melchizedek Priesthood. With the release of the house of Israel from Egyptian bondage, the Lord sought again to sanctify the people and bring them to the point of beholding his face and enjoying his presence (Exodus 19:7–11). But they rebelled, "hardened their hearts and could not endure his presence" (D&C 84:24). The loss that followed was catastrophic and lasted some twelve or thirteen hundred years, until the time of Jesus Christ:

> Therefore, he took Moses out of their midst, and the Holy Priesthood also;
>
> And the lesser priesthood continued, which priesthood holdeth the key of the ministering of angels and the preparatory gospel;
>
> Which gospel is the gospel of repentance and of baptism, and the remission of sins, and the law of carnal commandments, which the Lord in his wrath caused to continue with the house of Aaron among the children of Israel until John,

whom God raised up, being filled with the Holy Ghost from his mother's womb. (D&C 84:25–27)

The Joseph Smith Translation of Exodus 34:1 states that in addition to taking away the higher priesthood, the Lord took away his "holy order, and the ordinances thereof." Practically speaking, this means that the Mosaic Tabernacle, Solomon's Temple, and the later Temple of Herod did not administer the full range of the priesthood ordinances (including sealings performed by Melchizedek Priesthood officiators) to Israel as a whole. That is confirmed by President Joseph Fielding Smith:

> We are informed [D&C 124] that Moses was commanded to build a portable temple, generally called tabernacle, which could be carried with them in the wilderness. This tabernacle is the same temple where the boy Samuel heard the voice of the Lord. (1 Samuel, chapters one–three.) This sacred building was later replaced by Solomon's Temple. The question is often asked, 'What was the nature of the ordinances performed in these edifices in ancient times?' The Lord explains . . . that in ancient Israel they did not have the fulness of ordinances as we do today, and most, if not all, of which they were privileged to receive, very likely pertained to the Aaronic Priesthood. (See D. & C. 84:21–26.) Neither did the ancients labor in their temples for the salvation of the dead. That work was reserved until after the Savior's visit to the spirit world where he unlocked the door to the prison and had the gospel carried to the spirits who had been confined.[7]

Of course, all the prophets held the Melchizedek Priesthood, and specific individuals were privileged to receive all the associated ordinances. But Israel by and large was not so blessed, and most of the ordinances administered on a daily basis in the authorized temples were Aaronic Priesthood in nature and were performed by Aaronic priests, as described in the Old Testament.

The earthly ministry of Jesus Christ was a time of restoration. Jesus acted as the Elias of Restoration in his day, just as Joseph Smith acted as the Elias of Restoration in his (JST John 1:26–30). The Savior brought back not only the higher law and the higher priesthood to the house of Israel but also a knowledge of God the Father—knowledge that Israel as a whole was not privileged to comprehend. With the restoration of the higher law and the ordinances of the Melchizedek Priesthood, the early Church was established on a complete foundation, and disciples had every blessing available to them that operated during the period of the great patriarchs from Adam to Moses.

Sadly, the ordinances and blessings restored during the meridian dispensation were also lost through apostasy. The era of the Great Apostasy is really a function of the lack of authorized temples and associated priesthood ordinances as much as anything else. But following centuries without authorized temples, the fulness of the priesthood was again restored to this earth, and the house of Israel in modern times is again filling the temples of Jehovah. At some point, it seems reasonable to assume, the ancient Israelites who knew only the order of the Aaronic Priesthood will experience the ordinances of the fulness of the priesthood. This is the great work of the Millennium, and the anticipated proxy attendance in temples during the millennial era helps us to understand why we are preparing the earth with the dedication of new temples every year. President Brigham Young gave some idea of the number of temples we may expect to see during the Millennium: "To accomplish this work there will have to be not only one temple but thousands of them, and thousands and tens of thousands of men and women will go into those temples and officiate for people who have lived as far back as the Lord shall reveal."[8]

Regarding temple worship during the Millennium, President Joseph Fielding Smith gave us much to think about:

> During this time of peace, when the righteous shall come forth from their graves, they shall mingle with mortal men on the earth and instruct them. The veil which separates the living from the dead will be withdrawn and mortal men and the ancient saints shall converse together. Moreover, in perfect harmony shall they labor for the salvation and exaltation of the worthy who have died without the privileges of the gospel.
>
> The great work of the millennium shall be performed in the temples which shall cover all parts of the land and into which the children shall go to complete the work for their fathers, which they could not do when in this mortal life for themselves.
>
> In this manner those who have passed through the resurrection, and who know all about people and conditions on the other side, will place in the hands of those who are in mortality, the necessary information by and through which the great work of salvation for every worthy soul shall be performed, and thus the purposes of the Lord, as determined before the foundation of the world, will be fully consummated.[9]

It makes sense that temple worship and the Millennium go hand in hand. Temples symbolize peace, especially the

Prince of Peace. Temples belong to him. The Millennium is the great era of peace because it will be ruled over by the Prince of Peace, whose work will be completed in those houses dedicated to him.

An overarching lesson for us surely centers on the Lord's command to his disciples to build temples in every priesthood dispensation of his choosing. Though periods of rebellion and apostasy caused setbacks to the carrying out of the Father's plan of exaltation among his children and resulted in the loss of better temples than were sometimes built later, the plan moved forward. That was the case with the construction of Zerubbabel's Temple (515 B.C.) after the people of Israel returned to the holy land following their Babylonian captivity (586–538 B.C.). The shouting, singing, and praising that accompanied the completion of the foundation of the new temple were mingled with the laments of the older men—"many of the priests and Levites and chief of the fathers" (Ezra 3:12)—who had seen Solomon's Temple and therefore wept and wailed over the inferiority of the new house (Ezra 3:11–13).

New temples have been built, sometimes in the face of hardship and sometimes in the face of danger. But always there exists the drive to build houses of the Lord in these troubled dispensations. Apostasy, scattering, and the loss of temples have always been answered by restoration, gathering, and the construction of new temples. All of this great expenditure of human effort and resources is for the purpose of bringing the human family back into the presence of God the Father. Temples have always been symbols of the Father's love.

# 14

## A PROTECTION FOR
## THE SAINTS

*The temple is the place where all our missionary
labors culminate and are fulfilled; the temple protects and
orients all who attend—recent converts as well
as seasoned members.*

As a young full-time missionary, I was privileged to serve
with companions and leaders who believed the ultimate goal of our labors was not baptism but temple attendance. Many years have come and gone since those
days, and I am more convinced of that truth now than ever
before. Being worthy and able to enter the house of the Lord
is the greatest guide, protection, and resource a new member or returning prodigal has to help him or her remain on
the path leading back to our Father's presence.

Not long ago, I received an e-mail out of the blue from a
Church member I had not communicated with since my mission. The person asked if I was the full-time missionary who
had served in a certain area and helped teach a young couple
the missionary lessons; if so, did I know what had happened

to them? Yes, I was the missionary, but no, I did not know what had happened to the couple in the intervening years. I was present at their baptismal service but was transferred from the area immediately thereafter. In subsequent e-mail exchanges with this member, who was the next-door neighbor of the baptized couple (and their real teacher, I should add), I learned that one year after they were baptized, they were able, through diligent preparation, to attend the temple and be sealed as an eternal family by the power of the priesthood. Their sealing became an anchor to them. Both the husband and the wife had held responsible positions in their ward and stake and were now serving as missionaries themselves. They had blessed many lives.

I know this kind of story has been repeated many times throughout the world. I also know that the temple is a key factor, an anchor, in helping our Father's children live in a world spiraling downward at an accelerating rate and yet remain true to their covenants and stay optimistic about the future.

The ordinances performed within the sacred precincts of the temple bestow upon covenanters an endowment of power that can be duplicated nowhere else. The very temple itself, as well as its associated ordinances, "are as a refuge from life's storms—even a never-failing beacon guiding us to safety," President Thomas S. Monson has taught.[1] Elder Dennis B. Neuenschwander echoed those sentiments: "In holy places and in sacred space we find spiritual refuge, renewal, hope, and peace."[2] Temple ordinances inculcate a genuine optimism about the future.

Each temple is a holy, sacred place, a place of renewal,

hope, peace, and refuge where the Lord's Spirit can exist unrestrained. These blessings—the search for which has motivated honest truth-seekers to investigate the Lord's Church—are the very rewards offered to all seekers in richest measure in the temples of the Lord. Baptism and the gift of the Holy Ghost are tremendous gifts. They lead to the temple, where the door can be opened to the greatest gift the Father and the Son can give: exaltation or everlasting life in the family setting (D&C 6:13; 14:7).

The compelling environment of the temple will reach out and draw the pure in heart to its sacred precincts like iron to a magnet. Elder David B. Haight illustrated this truth with a story from the San Diego California Temple open house: "A devoted father lifted his frail fifteen-year-old daughter in his arms as he carried her from her wheelchair into the bride's dressing room. She looked around and said, 'Oh, this is so beautiful.' With a smile on her lips and with tears in her eyes, she gently laid her head on her father's shoulder and said, 'This is where I want to come to be married someday.' This young girl had come to the temple from the hospital, where she had spent most of the past five years—her wish to see the temple fulfilled."[3]

The temple provides the doctrinal basis and godly perspective for all that is taught and done in the Church. How critical a blessing it is for all of us, especially new members, to be able to see Church practices and policies from our Heavenly Father's perspective. That perspective, which we get from the temple, protects us from disenchantment, offense, or misunderstanding that can fester in our souls and take us out of the Church. The temple protects us by increasing our perspective on mortality as well as on eternity.

Teachings presented in the temple clearly identify the enemy of all righteousness, he who is the adversary of our Heavenly Father and the opponent of his plan. His name in premortality was Lucifer; he is now called Satan. (Remember, the Hebrew word *satan* means "adversary.") Temple teachings expose Satan's tactics: rebellion, ignorance, violence, tyranny, and the destruction of agency in this world. Temple teachings show us that we receive real protection against Satan and his tactics through the covenants we make in the Lord's house and live by in the fallen world. By keeping our covenants, we learn in a safe manner the wisdom of choosing good over evil, without having to suffer unnecessarily.

The temple and its ordinances protect each of us from the attacks of the adversary. The scriptures teach the profound truth that there is a natural enmity or hatred that exists between the kingdom of the world and the kingdom of God. The temple protects us from the prince of the kingdom of the world, Satan. The physical sanctuary of the temple allows us to leave the world and enter the safe environment of the Father's kingdom. Satan cannot enter the temple unless we bring him in. The temple and its ordinances strengthen our faith and give us courage to leave the sacred, protected environment of the temple and reenter the world until we can return to the temple the next time. The temple protects us by allowing us to make two-way promises called covenants, whereby the powers of heaven are called down on our behalf. We promise our loyalty to the Lord, promise to withhold nothing in coming to the aid of his kingdom, and he promises to come to us, to withhold no blessing in helping us conquer the adversary and overcome our problems and challenges, even the mightiest challenges. This is the greatest promise and protection in the universe.

At the dedication of the cornerstone of the Logan Temple, President George Q. Cannon taught the principle of power, protection, and assistance inherent in temples: "Every foundation stone that is laid for a Temple, and every Temple completed according to the order the Lord has revealed for his holy Priesthood, lessens the power of Satan on the earth, and increases the power of God and Godliness, moves the heavens in mighty power in our behalf, invokes and calls down upon us the blessings of the Eternal Gods, and those who reside in their presence."[4]

The temple orients and attunes every man and woman, every parent and grandparent to the family. And the temple stands as a bulwark to protect the family. President Howard W. Hunter reminded us that "in the ordinances of the temple, the foundations of the eternal family are sealed in place. The Church has the responsibility—and the authority—to preserve and protect the family as the foundation of society."[5]

Honoring our temple covenants protects us as individuals as well as families by keeping us safe from the devastating problems of immorality, divorce, disease, degradation, and the damaging of tender souls. Protection comes to individuals in many different ways as a result of the covenants, ordinances, and instructions received in the temple. President Joseph Fielding Smith testified of this:

> If we go into the temple, we raise our hands and covenant that we will serve the Lord and observe his

commandments and keep ourselves unspotted from the world. If we realize what we are doing, then the endowment will be a protection to us all our lives—a protection which a man who does not go to the temple does not have.

I have heard my father say that in the hour of trial, in the hour of temptation, he would think of the promises, the covenants that he had made in the house of the Lord, and they were a protection to him. He was but 15 years of age when he received his endowments and went forth into the mission field. This is exceptional, I know, and I do not recommend that our sons and our daughters go to the temple as young as that, but that they go as soon as they are prepared.

This protection is what these ceremonies are for, in part. They save us now, and they exalt us hereafter, if we will honor them. I know that this protection is given for I, too, have realized it, as have thousands of others who have remembered their obligations.[6]

The special clothing we make a covenant to wear when we leave the temple is also a tremendous protection to us in several ways—physically, spiritually, and symbolically—a bulwark against the enemy of our souls. President Carlos E. Asay reminded us that we are at war. Though our enemy is not an invading army, firing bullets at us or exploding bombs around us, we are, nevertheless, "engaged in a life-and-death struggle with forces capable of thrashing us inside out and sending us down into the depths of spiritual defeat if we are not vigilant."[7] That is why the apostle Paul counseled all disciples to "take unto you the whole armour of God, that ye may be able to withstand in the evil day, and having done all, to stand" (Ephesians 6:13). Doing all we can necessitates our going to the temple and putting on another kind of armor, as President Asay explained:

There is, however, another piece of armor worthy of our consideration. It is the special underclothing known as the temple garment, or garment of the holy priesthood, worn by members of The Church of Jesus Christ of Latter-day Saints who have received their temple endowment. This garment, worn day and night, serves three important purposes: it is a reminder of the sacred covenants made with the Lord in His holy house, a protective covering for the body, and a symbol of the modesty of dress and living that should characterize the lives of all the humble followers of Christ. . . .

The heavy armor worn by soldiers of a former day, including helmets, shields, and breastplates, determined the outcome of some battles. However, the real battles of life in our modern day will be won by those who are clad in a spiritual armor—an armor consisting of faith in God, faith in self, faith in one's cause, and faith in one's leaders. The piece of armor called the temple garment not only provides the comfort and warmth of a cloth covering, it also strengthens the wearer to resist temptation, fend off evil influences, and stand firmly for the right.[8]

When we understand the nature of the garment of the holy priesthood and what it does for us, wearing this special clothing becomes a privilege, a sacred privilege, extended to us by the Lord. It ceases to be an obligation and becomes a blessing and a protection. President Ezra Taft Benson reminded us: "When obedience ceases to be an irritant and becomes our quest, in that moment God will endow us with power."[9]

The Lord loves us and wants to shield us from lasting

harm, but he will not force us to accept his will. Therefore, he has given us the temple. President Packer explained:

> Sometimes our minds are so beset with problems, and there are so many things clamoring for attention at once that we just cannot think clearly and see clearly. At the temple the dust of distraction seems to settle out, the fog and the haze seem to lift, and we can "see" things that we were not able to see before and find a way through our troubles that we had not previously known.
>
> The Lord will bless us as we attend to the sacred ordinance work of the temples. Blessings there will not be limited to our temple service. We will be blessed in all of our affairs.[10]

The covenant path chosen by each member of The Church of Jesus Christ of Latter-day Saints—young or old, new or seasoned—comes as a result of following the promptings of the Holy Ghost. Because the Holy Ghost will lead every soul to all truth, the covenant path will eventually and ultimately lead to the temple. Within the walls of the temple the Holy Ghost can teach and testify "to the pure in heart in a manner that is unrestrained."[11] And I would add, in a manner unknowable to the world outside of the temple (see 1 Corinthians 2:11–15). The Holy Ghost provides to us a conduit of enlightenment and power to act in harmony with God's will. The gift of the Holy Ghost gives us the right and privilege of having that conduit open all of the time. The temple magnifies that conduit until our faith becomes knowledge and our enlightenment surpasses that of the angels.

The Lord declared, "That which is of God is light; and

he that receiveth light, and continueth in God, receiveth more light; and that light groweth brighter and brighter until the perfect day" (D&C 50:24). Surely this describes the path we embark upon when each of us is baptized. If we stay on that path by following the light of the Holy Ghost, we shall be filled with light until there is no darkness in us, until we comprehend all things, and "the days will come that [we] shall see him [God]" (D&C 88:68). The path that leads to this consummate manifestation goes through the temple, and that path is the goal of all of our missionary labors.

# 15

## SEALING FAMILIES BACK TO OUR FIRST PARENTS

*The temple is the center of missionary labor for those*
*who have passed on; it is the place of eternal linking where*
*the efforts of our family history research come to fruition.*

All our efforts to bring souls unto Christ, whether in mortality or in the spirit world, culminate in the temple. Elder Russell M. Nelson said, "Each temple is symbolic of our faith in God and an evidence of our faith in life after death. . . . All of our efforts in proclaiming the gospel, perfecting the Saints, and redeeming the dead lead to the holy temple."[1] Thus, the temple is the center and culmination of missionary activity among those who have temporarily put aside their mortal bodies. The gospel is being preached in the world of departed spirits by authorized ministers just as it is being taught in mortality. President Joseph F. Smith received a marvelous manifestation in 1918 in which he saw these missionary labors among the spirits in prison. "I beheld that the faithful elders of this dispensation, when they depart from mortal life, continue their labors in the preaching of the gospel of repentance and redemption, through the sacrifice of the Only Begotten Son of God, among those who are in darkness and under the bondage of sin in the great world of the spirits of the dead" (D&C 138:57).

He also saw that redemption comes *only* through the temple: "The dead who repent will be redeemed, through obedience to the ordinances of the house of God" (D&C 138:58).

The ordinances of salvation for the dead are indispensable, but they can only be performed on this earth by those possessing mortal bodies. President Spencer W. Kimball taught that "our great part in this aspect of missionary work is to perform on this earth the ordinances required for those who accept the gospel over there [the spirit world]."[2]

There is no doctrine that Joseph Smith thought was more important or better supported in scripture than salvation for the dead. Said he: "This doctrine presents in a clear light the wisdom and mercy of God in preparing an ordinance for the salvation of the dead, being baptized by proxy, their names recorded in heaven and they judged according to the deeds done in the body. This doctrine was the burden of the scriptures. Those Saints who neglect it in behalf of their deceased relatives, do it at the peril of their own salvation."[3]

Joseph spoke about salvation for the dead numerous times. On one occasion, at the request of the Quorum of the Twelve, the Prophet gave instructions on the doctrine of baptism for the dead and presented it "as the only way that men can appear as saviors on Mount Zion."[4] On another

occasion he gave tremendous insight into the biblical doctrine of becoming saviors on Mount Zion:

> The Bible says, "I will send you Elijah the Prophet before
> the coming of the great and dreadful day of the Lord; and he
> shall turn the heart of the fathers to the children, and the
> heart of the children to the fathers, lest I come and smite the
> earth with a curse."
>
> Now, the word *turn* here should be translated *bind,* or
> seal. But what is the object of this important mission? or how
> is it to be fulfilled? The keys are to be delivered, the spirit of
> Elijah is to come, the Gospel to be established, the Saints of
> God gathered, Zion built up, and the Saints to come up as
> saviors on Mount Zion.
>
> But how are they to become saviors on Mount Zion? By
> building their temples, erecting their baptismal fonts, and
> going forth and receiving all the ordinances, baptisms, con-
> firmations, washing, anointings, ordinations and sealing pow-
> ers upon their heads, in behalf of all their progenitors who
> are dead, and redeem them that they may come forth in the
> first resurrection and be exalted to thrones of glory with
> them; and herein is the chain that binds the hearts of the
> fathers to the children, and the children to the fathers,
> which fulfills the mission of Elijah.[5]

That is how the eternal linking of generations takes
place, the creation of "the chain that binds." It is through
the sealing power of the priesthood, which the living make
available to the dead. Joseph's prophetic commentary also
gives valuable clarification to Malachi 4:5–6 and Doctrine
and Covenants 2. The word *turn* should be translated "bind"
or "seal." Elijah would return to bind or seal the hearts of

parents and children to each other through the priesthood he restored prior to the Second Coming.

Joseph Smith's immediate successors did not retreat from making known the importance of this doctrine, themselves having been tutored by the Prophet and by the Lord. President Brigham Young taught that one of the greatest responsibilities we have as mortals is to ensure that temple ordinances are performed for those who have died, so that the chain of generations can be welded together:

> We are called, as it has been told you, to redeem the nations of the earth. The fathers cannot be made perfect without us; we cannot be made perfect without the fathers. There must be this chain in the holy Priesthood; it must be welded together from the latest generation that lives on the earth back to Father Adam, to bring back all that can be saved and placed where they can receive salvation and a glory in some kingdom. This Priesthood has to do it; this Priesthood is for this purpose. . . .
>
> The doctrines of the Savior reveal and place the believers in possession of principles whereby saviors will come upon Mount Zion to save . . . all except those who have sinned against the Holy Ghost. Men and women will enter into the temples of God, and be, in comparison, pillars there [see Revelation 3:12], and officiate year after year for those who have slept thousands of years.[6]

President Young noted that already in his day members of the Church, as well as those of other faiths, were being touched by the Lord's Spirit in such a way as to become almost obsessed with the desire to search out their ancestors: "The Lord is stirring up the hearts of many . . . and there is a perfect mania with some to trace their genealogies and to get up printed records of their ancestors. They do not know what they are doing it for, but the Lord is prompting them; and it will continue and run on from father to father, father to father, until they get the genealogy of their forefathers as far as they possibly can."[7]

President Young stressed that we have an obligation to search our family histories back as far as we can. At the point where we can go no farther, we are entitled to the help of heaven. He spoke of a time when "the servants of God who have lived on the earth in ages past will reveal where different persons have lived who have died without the Gospel, give their names, and say, 'Now go forth, ye servants of God, and exercise your rights and privileges; go and perform the ordinances of the house of God for those who have passed their probation without the Gospel.'"[8]

Furthermore, President Young prophesied that in a future day someone in the temple would step forward and say:

> Somebody came to the temple last night; we did not know who he was, but he was no doubt a brother, and told us a great many things we did not before understand. He gave us the names of a great many of our forefathers that are not on record, and he gave me my true lineage and the names of my forefathers for hundreds of years back. He said to me, you and I are connected in one family; there are the names of your ancestors; take them and write them down, and be baptized and confirmed, and save such and such ones, and receive of the blessings of the eternal Priesthood for such and such an individual, as you do for yourselves.[9]

The days when the miracles spoken of by President

Young are upon us. I have spoken with individuals who have experienced the fulfillment of his promises. One friend wrote:

> In the last couple of weeks . . . , that miracle described by President Young occurred in our lives. . . . In my case, a total "stranger," a nonmember, but as I have since learned, an actual relative, came forward over the internet with all these names. Maybe it wasn't an angel or someone beyond the veil, but I am convinced that my ancestors, long dead, moved heaven and earth to establish the relationship I now have with this newly-found Dutch 11th "cousin." He says that his passion for genealogy was a hobby, but clearly the Spirit of Elijah moved upon him years ago, and with the promptings of my family beyond the veil, and with the miracle of computers, we met each other in cyberspace. In the near future, as the temple work is done, my ancestors will finally be free of the "chains" that bound them for centuries and they will be able to move on in their progress to exaltation and eternal lives.[10]

The Internet is a miracle and the Lord's invention to hasten his work in our day. It is part of the help from heaven promised in our day. Through its operations it is as though angels and ancestors beyond the grave are able to step forward, as President Young prophesied, and tell us things we did not understand as well as give us the names of forefathers long forgotten. In my own case, miracles have happened and people have stepped forward as President Young said they would. I have had the help of heaven.

The age of miracles and manifestations pertaining to missionary and temple work for the dead is just beginning.

Consider the testimony of Archibald F. Bennett, a prominent genealogist:

> Sister Susa Young Gates . . . once asked her father [Brigham Young] how it would ever be possible to accomplish the great amount of temple work that must be done, if all are given a full opportunity for exaltation. He told her there would be many inventions of labor-saving devices, so that our daily duties could be performed in a short time, leaving us more and more time for temple work. The inventions have come, and are still coming, but many simply divert the time gained to other channels, and not for the purpose intended by the Lord.[11]

Our vicarious efforts in the temple are the culmination of all the missionary labors in the spirit world, just as the temple is the desired culmination of our missionary labors here in mortality. These activities are cut from the same cloth, part of the same plan. President Spencer W. Kimball gave us a prophet's perspective: "The more clearly we see eternity, the more obvious it becomes that the Lord's work . . . is one vast and grand work with striking similarities on each side of the veil."[12]

The Lord's plan of salvation for both the living and the dead is so stunning because it is so huge—involving such large numbers of human beings. Christian theologians of other denominations have wrestled in ignorance with the questions that temple worship answers: "What is the fate of those who die never hearing the gospel of Christ? Are all the 'heathen' lost? Is there an opportunity for those who have never heard of Jesus to be saved?"[13] These very questions, articulated by a Christian not of our faith, are in the forefront of theological debate in some circles, and, according to him, constitute "one of the most perplexing, provocative and perennial issues facing Christians. . . . Far and away, this is the most-asked apologetic question [i.e., the final destiny of those dying without knowledge of Jesus] on U.S. college campuses."[14]

The problem is all the more vexing because of the sheer magnitude of it:

> A large proportion of the human race has died without ever hearing the good news of Jesus. It is estimated that in A.D. 100 there were 181 million people, of whom 1 million were Christians. It is also believed there were 60,000 unreached people groups at that time. By the year 1000 there were 270 million people, 50 million of whom were Christians, with 50,000 unreached people groups. In 1989 there were 5.2 billion people, with 1.7 billion Christians and 12,000 unreached people groups. In addition we could think of all those who lived prior to [the birth of Christ] who never heard of the Israelites and God's covenant with them. Although there is no way of knowing exactly how many people died without ever hearing about Israel or the church, it seems safe to conclude that the vast majority of human beings who have ever lived fall into this category.
>
> In terms of sheer numbers, then, an inquiry into the salvation of the unevangelized is of immense interest. What may be said about the destiny of countless billions who have lived and died apart from any understanding of the divine grace manifested in Jesus?[15]

Most Christians do not have a good answer to this legitimate question. And though they should not be chided in the slightest or held in derision for it, there are a few experts who refuse to countenance LDS doctrine, because if they did, they would have to reexamine and revamp their whole theological framework. Consider one example: "My point is that the [Post Mortem Evangelization] reading of 1 Peter 4:6 is neither the only nor even the most plausible interpretation. Wise Christians do not base any important doctrine—especially one that is controversial and that might also contain heretical implications—on one single, highly debatable passage of Scripture. If this approach were applied . . . to 1 Corinthians 15:29, it would lead Christians to follow a policy of baptizing living people as proxies for the unbaptized dead."[16]

Indeed. Despite his protestations, we wonder if this author does not in truth recognize even faint connections between 1 Peter 4:6 and 1 Corinthians 15:29 as well as 1 Peter 3:18–19. At any rate, Latter-day Saints can rejoice over such revelations as Doctrine and Covenants 138, which weave together the various doctrines of the plan of exaltation into the seamless fabric of truth, saving us from wandering in the dark and preventing us from being tossed about by every wind of doctrine devised by the sleight of men (Ephesians 4:14).

There is an inspired answer to questions regarding the fate of those who have not heard this gospel. And it is what Joseph Smith revealed in the early days of the Restoration:

> All those who have not had an opportunity of hearing the Gospel, and being administered unto by an inspired man in the flesh, must have it hereafter, before they can be finally judged.[17]

What promises are made in relation to the subject of the salvation of the dead? and what kind of characters are those who can be saved, although their bodies are mouldering and decaying in the grave? When His commandments teach us, it is in view of eternity; for we are looked upon by God as though we were in eternity. God dwells in eternity, and does not view things as we do.

The greatest responsibility in this world that God has laid upon us is to seek after our dead. The Apostle says, "They without us cannot be made perfect;" (Hebrews 11:40) for it is necessary that the sealing power should be in our hands to seal our children and our dead for the fulness of the dispensation of times—a dispensation to meet the promises made by Jesus Christ before the foundation of the world for the salvation of man.[18]

President Joseph F. Smith revealed to us, through his vision of the spirit world, the exultation that broke forth in that place when the Savior made his appearance and declared deliverance and "liberty to the captives who had been faithful" (D&C 138:18). He then authorized his servants to go forth to preach the gospel in the rest of the spirit world. Can we even begin to imagine what rejoicing occurs, what tears of joy are shed, when those in the spirit world who died without the gospel, perhaps even believing that God has forgotten them, hear their names spoken for the first time in hundreds or even thousands of years when we stand as proxies in their stead in the Lord's house? Some of them probably were forgotten or ignored while in mortality, living hard, impoverished, pedestrian existences. But in God's holy house, we help to show to those spirits in prison that he has not forgotten them. He has not forsaken them. He knows them by name! When we enter the temple and speak the names of the deceased as though they themselves were making the covenants of eternity, we make it possible for them to be set free. As Elder David B. Haight said, "Regular temple attendance is one of the simplest ways you can bless those who are waiting in the spirit world. . . . If you will do this, you will know the indescribable joy of being a savior on Mount Zion to a waiting ancestor whom you have helped."[19] When we enter the Lord's holy house we act as partners with the Father and the Son, declaring that God loves and remembers all of his children as specific individuals.

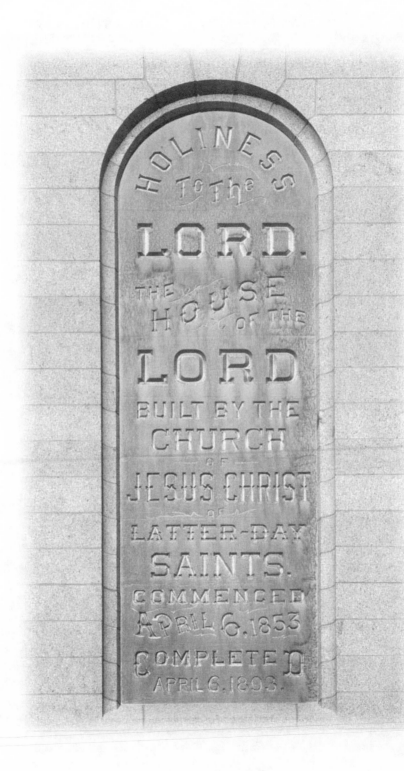

# 16

## WORTHINESS TO ENTER THE HOUSE OF THE LORD

*Dedicated temples are, in every sense,*
*the house of the Lord, and those who enter the home*
*of the Master as guests must be worthy!*

Several years ago, as a young man called to full-time missionary service, I found myself in the old Mission Home
in Salt Lake City, just north of the temple. We ate our meals
in the basement of the Hotel Utah (now the Joseph Smith
Memorial Building). One evening as my companion and I
walked around the corner, heading for the Mission Home
after supper, we were startled to see the temple all lit up—
truly aglow. I suppose it had been lit up before, but I had
never noticed. We stopped to gaze at the lettering, written in
gold, high up on the east face of that holy sanctuary:
"HOLINESS TO THE LORD—THE HOUSE OF THE LORD." I was
mesmerized by the sight. I catalogued it in my mind and
went on my way. Two days later I was in that temple, attend-
ing a special session with the other missionaries in our group.
We were seated quietly on the fourth floor of the temple,

waiting for President Harold B. Lee to instruct us. When he entered we stood to honor a senior apostle of Jesus Christ, and the Spirit of the Lord intensified in the large room. The experience was physical as well as spiritual in its impact.

At a certain point, President Lee invited questions. We were told that because we were in the temple we could ask any question we desired about the temple, its ordinances, or the gospel in general. My associates and I were impressed with President Lee's ability to answer every question from the scriptures, which he had with him. A question was asked, and I remember this spiritual giant saying, "Well, let's see what the Lord has to say about the matter." He would then read a passage from the standard works that answered the question. I also remember thinking that I wanted to be able to do that someday. Of course, the pity of the whole situation was that I did not even know enough to ask a question.

I do, however, remember one question with clarity. President Lee called upon a young elder, probably my age. He stood and said: "On the outside of the temple it says this is the house of the Lord. Do you think he has ever been here?" I did not then realize how bold a question that really was. As a nineteen year old, overwhelmed by all I had experienced those last few days, I thought it was a pretty good one. President Lee closed his scriptures, put them aside, looked at the young missionary, and said (as nearly as I can recollect): "Oh, elder, do not ask if he has ever been here. This is his house—and he walks these very halls."

It was a dramatic moment. It was as though an electric shock jolted me. I had never heard such a thing before.

President Lee's answer was nothing less than arresting. I did not hear anything else that transpired, or at least I do not remember what else happened. "He walks these very halls." That statement shaped my feelings about the temple from that day onward. I do not take lightly, or view as metaphor, statements such as the one from Elder Russell M. Nelson: "A temple is literally the house of the Lord."[1]

Several accounts may be found describing visits by the Lord to individuals in mortality, but none is a better second witness to President Lee's testimony than the account of Allie Young Pond, granddaughter of President Lorenzo Snow. She related the following:

> One evening while I was visiting Grandpa Snow in his room in the Salt Lake Temple, I remained until the doorkeepers had gone and the night-watchmen had not yet come in, so grandpa said he would take me to the main front entrance and let me out that way. He got his bunch of keys from his dresser. After we left his room, and while we were still in the large corridor leading into the celestial room, I was walking several steps ahead of grandpa when he stopped me, and said: "Wait a moment, Allie. I want to tell you something. It was right here that the Lord Jesus Christ appeared to me at the time of the death of President Woodruff. He instructed me to go right ahead and reorganize the First Presidency of the Church at once and not wait as had been done after the death of the previous presidents, and that I was to succeed President Woodruff."
>
> Then grandpa came a step nearer and held out his left hand and said: "He stood right here, about three feet above the floor. It looked as though he stood on a plate of solid gold."

Grandpa told me what a glorious personage the Savior is and described His hands, feet, countenance and beautiful white robes, all of which were of such a glory of whiteness and brightness that he could hardly gaze upon Him.

Then he came another step nearer and put his right hand on my head and said: "Now, granddaughter, I want you to remember that this is the testimony of your grandfather, that he told you with his own lips that he actually saw the Savior, here in the Temple and talked with Him face to face."[2]

Indeed, the Savior walks the halls of his holy house. Heaven is nearer than some of us imagine. But this should not surprise students of the Doctrine and Covenants. In a revelation given to Joseph Smith in 1833, the Lord makes an exhilarating promise regarding the temple: "And inasmuch as my people build a house unto me in the name of the Lord, and do not suffer any unclean thing to come into it, that it be not defiled, my glory shall rest upon it; yea, and my presence shall be there, for I will come into it, and all the pure in heart that shall come into it shall see God. But if it be defiled I will not come into it, and my glory shall not be there; for I will not come into unholy temples" (D&C 97:15–17).

What a promise! These are not idle words: "all the pure in heart that shall come into it [the temple] shall see God." Consider this declaration, also given in 1833: "Verily, thus saith the Lord: It shall come to pass that every soul who forsaketh his sins and cometh unto me, and calleth on my name, and obeyeth my voice, and keepeth my commandments, shall see my face and know that I am" (D&C 93:1).

In 1836 at the dedication of the Kirtland Temple, the first in this last dispensation, the Prophet Joseph Smith prayed that the temple would be "sanctified and consecrated to be holy" so that the Lord's "holy presence [could] be continually" in his house (D&C 109:12). Other temples built since that time have been similarly dedicated and supernal promises extended to all who enter them. We may come into the presence of the Lord if we are clean when we enter his holy house, so that it remains undefiled.

Because Latter-day Saint temples possess the same degree of sanctity and holiness as ancient temples—where the Lord appeared—the same degree of worthiness is required of every invited guest today as anciently. Consider the standard set forth in Ezekiel 44:9: "Thus saith the Lord God; No stranger, uncircumcised in heart, nor uncircumcised in flesh, shall enter into my sanctuary, of any stranger that is among the children of Israel." Just as ancient Israel could not, by divine decree, allow any strangers to enter God's holy home, so too modern Israel, by divine decree, cannot allow any stranger to enter God's holy home. Wealth or worldly position count for nothing if individuals are not recognized as legitimate invited guests by the Master of the house or his authorized servants.

Recognized guests in modern times are those who have been certified in worthiness through the interview process conducted by authorized servants of Jesus Christ. During the times I served as a bishop and a branch president, it was impressed on me again and again that I was a guardian of the temple to protect it from desecration. Perhaps that is why Elder Nelson's words mean so much to me:

Judges in Israel who hold keys of priesthood authority and responsibility help us prepare [to attend the temple] by conducting temple recommend interviews. These leaders care for us and help us determine if we are ready to attend the temple. They also love the Lord and ensure "that no unclean thing shall be permitted to come into [His] house." Thus, these interviews are conducted in a spirit of accountability. . . .

The requirements are simple. Succinctly stated, an individual is required to keep the commandments of Him whose house it is. He has set the standards. We enter the temple as His guests.

President Hinckley said, "I urge our people everywhere, with all of the persuasiveness of which I am capable, to live worthy to hold a temple recommend, to secure one and regard it as a precious asset, and to make a greater effort to go to the house of the Lord and partake of the spirit and the blessings to be had therein."

The Lord would be pleased if every adult member would be worthy of—and carry—a current temple recommend. "Interviews . . . for temple recommends, with your bishop and members of your stake presidency are precious experiences. And, in a way, they could be considered meaningful 'dress rehearsals' for that grand colloquy when you will stand before the Great Judge."[3]

Truly, the temple recommend is both a symbol of our commitment to the Father and the Son and a pattern of the final judgment, when we "stand before the Great Judge," as Elder Nelson said. I have been taught by saintly people just how valuable a temple recommend is, what it stands for, and how I ought to regard it. One of our family's dear friends told us of going to a temple recommend interview with his dying father-in-law. Our friend was there to interpret for his father-in-law, who did not speak English but wanted to be sure to have his current recommend with him when the end came. A little later, just before the lid of his father-in-law's casket was closed for the final time, our friend slipped the renewed recommend into the shirt pocket of his father-in-law. It was the last act of love to be performed on this earth before the two would meet again in the spirit world and on the day of resurrection.

As temple recommend holders, part of our charge to keep the temple pure and undefiled is to keep all ordinances, covenants, and instructions sacred and unsullied by not exposing them to public scrutiny or scorn. Base, spiritually insensitive individuals who sometimes look for things to ridicule are hardly the ones qualified to sit in judgment of the Lord's holy and higher ways (see Isaiah 55:8–9).

The temple recommend is a symbol of the things that matter most—our worthiness to enter the literal home of the Lord on earth and someday to enter his physical presence. It is a symbol of our certainty of the reality of the Resurrection. In a way, a temple recommend is a passport to the best, most desirable part of that unseen, but real, world awaiting all of us. Securing a temple recommend through careful preparation in worthiness is one way we prepare for the journey ahead. When I look at my recommend now, I often think back on that amazing moment so many years ago in the Salt Lake Temple and the words of President Lee: "Oh, elder, do not ask if he has ever been here. This is his house—and he walks these very halls."

# 17

## A PORTAL TO HEAVEN

*The temple is a portal to heaven,*
*where many righteous beings from the unseen*
*world may be felt, or heard, or seen.*

In the temple, the veil separating mortals from heavenly beings becomes very, very thin. Not only does the Savior visit his temples, but other beings from the unseen world may contact mortals who are involved in temple ministrations.

Heavenly beings minister to mortals for various reasons. One is to establish faith in God and reaffirm to humankind hope in the power and glory of Deity (Alma 12:28–30). Another reason is to testify of Jesus Christ. Mormon wrote: "God . . . sent angels to minister unto the children of men, to make manifest concerning the coming of Christ; and in Christ there should come every good thing" (Moroni 7:22). Still another reason is to call people to repentance and to prepare ministers of the Savior's gospel so that they may teach others. Speaking specifically of the ministry of angels,

Mormon said: "And the office of their ministry is to call men unto repentance, and to fulfill and to do the work of the covenants of the Father, . . . to prepare the way among the children of men, by declaring the word of Christ unto the chosen vessels of the Lord, that they may bear testimony of him" (Moroni 7:31). Whatever else might be said, it is critical to remember that heavenly beings (resurrected angels and unembodied spirits) are subject unto Christ and always interact with mortals "to minister according to the word of his command," to fulfill his divine purposes (Moroni 7:30).

The Prophet Joseph Smith indicated that the Kirtland Temple, the first completed in this dispensation, was built specifically so the Saints could receive divine manifestations, be taught from on high, and be endowed with power. Already by 1831 the Lord had instructed: "Sanctify yourselves and ye shall be endowed with power" (D&C 43:16). In another revelation given at Kirtland, Ohio, in 1833, the Lord reiterated the promise of an endowment of power and reconfirmed the command to build the temple where that endowment would be given: "I gave unto you a commandment that you should build a house, in the which house I design to endow those whom I have chosen with power from on high; for this is the promise of the Father unto you; therefore I command you to tarry, even as mine apostles at Jerusalem" (D&C 95:8–9).

This is exactly what the gospel of Luke reports as having happened; the ancient apostles were commanded to tarry at Jerusalem. But what is sometimes overlooked is that Jesus' command in the New Testament was given in the context of the Jerusalem Temple: "And, behold, I send the promise of my Father upon you: but tarry ye in the city of Jerusalem, until ye be endued with power from on high. . . . And they worshipped him, and returned to Jerusalem with great joy: and were continually in the temple, praising and blessing God. Amen" (Luke 24:49, 52–53).

It is significant that Luke records this last scene in his gospel because he is the one who describes events on the day of Pentecost in the sequel to his Gospel, the Acts of the Apostles (chapter 2). Pentecost was a temple-connected event.

In May 1834 Oliver Cowdery harkened back to the connection between the temple and Pentecost when he wrote in anticipation of the Kirtland Temple being finished: "Within that house, God will pour out his Spirit in great majesty and glory, and encircle his people with fire more gloriously and marvelously than at Pentecost, because the work to be performed in the last days is greater than was in that day."[1]

Oliver's statement was prophetic in two ways. First, he wrote to John F. Boynton of Saco, Maine, on behalf of the presidency of the Church. Second, what he predicted came true. Weeks and even months before the dedication of the Kirtland Temple the Lord poured out on the Saints his holy Spirit, including visions, manifestations, heavenly appearances, and endowments of divine power. From January 21 to May 1 of 1836, in the temple, "probably more Latter-day Saints beheld visions and witnessed other unusual spiritual manifestations than during any other era in the history of the Church," said Professor Milton Backman of Brigham Young University.[2] The first temple in this dispensation set the pattern for the future in a magnificent and dramatic way.

One of the first manifestations within the Kirtland Temple was also one of the most significant. It occurred on Thursday, January 21, 1836. Joseph Smith recorded that

> at early candle-light I met with the Presidency at the west school room, in the Temple, to attend to the ordinance of anointing our heads with holy oil. . . . We then laid our hands upon our aged Father Smith, and invoked the blessings of heaven. . . . The heavens were opened upon us, and I beheld the celestial kingdom of God, and the glory thereof. . . . I saw . . . the blazing throne of God. . . . I saw the beautiful streets of that kingdom, which had the appearance of being paved with gold.[3]

This revelation, of course, has been canonized as Doctrine and Covenants 137. In addition, the Prophet said:

> Many of my brethren who received the ordinance [of washing and anointing] with me saw glorious visions also. Angels ministered unto them as well as to myself, and the power of the Highest rested upon us, the house was filled with the glory of God, and we shouted Hosanna to God and the Lamb. . . . Some of them saw the face of the Savior, . . . for we all communed with the heavenly host.[4]

Probably the best-known manifestations in the Kirtland Temple are those associated with its dedication, held Sunday, March 27, 1836, and later the solemn assembly. The Prophet had been encouraging the faithful to prepare for the glorious endowment of godly power and blessings that Deity had in store for them. The Twelve especially were admonished to "prepare their hearts in all humility for an endowment with power from on high."[5] The Prophet understood that preparation precedes power.

Therefore, even before the temple was finished, Joseph administered some of the ordinances of the house of the Lord to several of the brethren in order to prepare their minds and hearts to receive the magnificent manifestations that occurred during the period of the Kirtland Temple dedication and subsequent solemn assembly, and which are now part of the historical record.

As Brigham Young explained, these ordinances administered by Joseph Smith at Kirtland were not the full endowment or temple ceremony later given to the Saints in the Nauvoo Temple but rather consisted of "some of the first, or introductory, or initiatory ordinances, preparatory to an endowment."[6] Elder Erastus Snow indicates that the number who received these preparatory blessings "in the house of the Lord in Kirtland was about three hundred and sixty."[7] These introductory ordinances established a fitting environment that invited the manifestations of heaven and the great spiritual power that descended upon the Saints at that time. This ought to be a great lesson to us. Maybe we ought to do all within our power to make sure our young people and new converts begin to prepare themselves early to attend the temple in order to be ready for greater things to come.

Early on the morning of March 27, many hundreds of people had gathered outside the temple, hoping to attend the service in anticipation of the bestowal of promised blessings. The temple doors were opened at 8:00 A.M. The First Presidency assisted with seating, and the temple was soon filled to overflowing—almost a thousand individuals—and the doors were closed. This left hundreds of people still out-side, including several who had made great sacrifices for the temple's construction and many who had traveled significant distances. Therefore, the Prophet directed that the dedica-tory service be repeated the following Thursday for their benefit.

The Sunday dedicatory service began at 9:00 A.M. and lasted until 4:00 P.M. True to his word and commensurate with the preparation of the faithful, the Lord gave those in attendance divine manifestations and bestowed endowments of power. President Frederick G. Williams testified that while President Sidney Rigdon was making his first prayer, an angel entered through the window and sat between him and Father Smith.[8] "David Whitmer also saw angels in the house."[9] The evening of the dedication, Joseph Smith met with quorums of priesthood holders in the temple. He encouraged them not to fear, not to quench the Spirit, but to receive the Spirit of prophecy. The following then occurred:

> Brother George A. Smith arose and began to prophesy, when a noise was heard like the sound of a rushing mighty wind, which filled the Temple, and all the congregation simultaneously arose, being moved upon by an invisible power; many began to speak in tongues and prophesy; oth-ers saw glorious visions; and I beheld the Temple was filled with angels, which fact I declared to the congregation. The people of the neighborhood came running together (hearing an unusual sound within, and seeing a bright light like a pil-lar of fire resting upon the Temple), and were astonished at what was taking place. This continued until the meeting closed at eleven P.M.[10]

The parallel between events that night in Kirtland and the events of Pentecost some eighteen hundred years earlier are unmistakable. But that was only one of many more divine manifestations that were experienced in the temple during that period in early 1836. Benjamin Brown attended many of the meetings held in the temple at that time. He testified that the Spirit of God was "profusely poured out." Said he: "We had a most glorious and never-to-be-forgotten time. Angels were seen by numbers present."[11] Heber C. Kimball also reported the ministry of angels and manifestations such as those reported on the day of Pentecost in the New Testament times. He said, "This continued several days. . . . During this time many great and marvelous visions were seen."[12]

Many more episodes from the Kirtland Temple period could be marshaled to confirm the truth that temples are the portals of heaven, the gathering places of beings from the unseen world. Kirtland was the prototype, and in some ways the epitome, but it was not unique.

President Wilford Woodruff testified of some remarkable, now famous, experiences in which he participated personally in the St. George Temple:

> I will here say . . . that two weeks before I left St. George, the spirits of the dead gathered around me, wanting to know why we did not redeem them. Said they, "You have had the use of the Endowment House for a number of years, and yet nothing has ever been done for us. We laid the foundation of the government you now enjoy, and we never apostatized from it, but we remained true to it and were faithful to God. . . . I straightway went into the baptismal font and called

upon Brother McAllister to baptize me for the signers of the
Declaration of Independence, and fifty other eminent men,
making one hundred in all, including John Wesley,
Columbus, and others.[13]

Twenty years later, in general conference, the experience
was still fresh in his mind:

Every one of those men that signed the Declaration of
Independence, with General Washington, called upon me,
as an Apostle of the Lord Jesus Christ, in the Temple at St.
George, two consecutive nights, and demanded at my hands
that I should go forth and attend to the ordinances of the
House of God for them. . . . I told these brethren that it was
their duty to go into the Temple and labor until they had got
endowments for all of them. They did it. Would those spirits
have called upon me, as an elder in Israel, to perform that
work if they had not been noble spirits before God? They
would not.[14]

James G. Bleak, chief recorder of the St. George Temple,
was a second witness to President Woodruff's initial
visitations:

I was also present in the St. George Temple and witnessed the appearance of the Spirits of the Signers . . . the
spirits of the Presidents. . . . And also others, such as Martin
Luther and John Wesley. . . . [w]ho came to Wilford
Woodruff and demanded that their baptism and endowments be done. Wilford Woodruff was baptized for all of
them. While I and Brothers J. D. T. McAllister and David H.
Cannon (who were witnesses to the request) were endowed
for them. These men . . . laid the foundation of this
American Gov., and signed the Declaration of Independence

and were the best spirits the God of Heaven could find on the face of the earth to perform this work. Martin Luther and John Wesley helped to release the people from religious bondage that held them during the dark ages. They also prepared the peoples hearts so they would be ready to receive the restored gospel when the Lord sent it again to men on the earth.[15]

Closer to our own day, we can point to the Nauvoo Temple. While the original edifice was not noted by contemporary Church leaders as a place of great manifestations and visitations, the rebuilt Nauvoo Illinois Temple began its service hosting heavenly visitors. At the dedication of the temple in June 2002, President Gordon B. Hinckley shared with us some powerful insights into how closely heaven was looking in on the dedication services. Early in the day, at the cornerstone ceremony, President Hinckley said: "I intend to say in the dedicatory services that there will be with us today an unseen audience, and that Joseph and Hyrum Smith will be in that audience and many others."[16]

True to his promise, President Hinckley spoke of heavenly visitors in the dedicatory services: "I am *sure* there is a great unseen audience looking upon us, those who passed to the other side and see in the structure which we dedicate today a fulfillment of their hopes, their dreams, and some compensation for their tears and their indescribable sacrifices."[17] And if that weren't enough, President Hinckley also said that he "felt the presence of the Father and the Son, 'who have revealed Themselves to the Prophet Joseph who gave his life for this work. I think *he* must rejoice.'"[18]

These kinds of interactions and manifestations, while

dramatic and well known and more the exception than the rule, are nonetheless not reserved for Church presidents only. Other faithful members of the Lord's Church can and have enjoyed the impressions of the Spirit of the Lord, and even the audible voice or visible manifestation of beings from the unseen world in the temple. A few years ago, my wife, Janet, and I were privileged to be in the Nauvoo Illinois Temple. As I was waiting for her, I had the good fortune of speaking with one of the sealers who attended the dedication service. I said to him how wonderful it must have been to be there and hear President Hinckley express the feelings and impressions he had. He then tried to tell me of some personal feelings he had. All he could say was that he knew for himself that heavenly choirs were in attendance in the temple.

Members of my family have had sacred revelatory experiences in the temple with beings from the other side of the veil and have so testified. One aunt, whose husband has been deceased for almost forty years, has been in the temple on special occasions involving their children and grandchildren. One time, wishing her eternal companion could be there to witness the sublime moment, she was inspired to call out in her mind's voice, "Dale, are you here?" In a large family gathering she recounted the special feeling that overcame her, as she heard the voice of her husband saying, "Yes, I am here, and so are others [members of the family]!" Beings of the unseen world are real.

Truly, dedicated temples of the Lord are portals to heaven. The veil is very thin in them. On occasion beings from the other side of the veil have appeared. But always the

Holy Spirit is there. Though we do not need dramatic visual manifestations to know of the reality of the unseen world and heavenly beings, we do need the Holy Ghost. We need a worthy mind and heart to recognize the revelations that come from heaven to us in the temple. At Kirtland, Milo Andrus approached Joseph Smith and indicated (complained) that he had not been the recipient of any of the dramatic manifestations witnessed at the temple dedicatory services. He came away from that interview resolved to be worthy of revelation, and when he did experience the power of the Holy Ghost and saw fire descend on the Elders after prayer, fasting, and worthy living, he exclaimed: "It is enough, O Father, I will bear a faithful testimony of it while I live."[19] And so he did.

I think some of us are like Milo Andrus. We must prepare in worthiness to recognize the thoughts, promptings, whisperings, and impressions that come from heaven through the portal we call the temple (and I believe such things will inevitably come to the faithful). Then we may feel to exclaim, "It is enough . . . I will bear a faithful testimony of it [the power of the Holy Ghost] while I live."

# 18

## A PLACE OF PERSONAL
## REVELATION AND EDUCATION

*Because the temple is a portal to heaven,*
*it is a place of personal revelation and education—*
*the Lord's perfect university.*

The environment of the temple invites revelation. It is instructive that Joseph Smith received his vision of the celestial kingdom (D&C 137) while he was physically within the walls of the Kirtland Temple on January 21, 1836. The Prophet did not offer any explanation, personal feeling, or commentary on this stunning vision wherein he witnessed his yet-living mother and father among the exalted, enjoying eternity in the Father's presence. But surely we do not miss the point that the temple, even the physical space of the unfinished temple, provided the necessary environment for the Prophet's remarkable experience. The deaths of Joseph's parents—his father's in 1840 and his mother's in 1856—take on a different perspective against the backdrop of the glorious vision and promises of 1836. Now we see that death allows the fulfillment of awaiting blessings. Lesson: Things look different in the context of the information provided in the temple. The temple educates us on eternity.

President Gordon B. Hinckley has testified of the revelatory environment of the temple: "The temple is also a place of personal inspiration and revelation. Legion are those who in times of stress, when difficult decisions must be made and perplexing problems must be handled, have come to the temple in a spirit of fasting and prayer to seek divine direction. Many have testified that while voices of revelation were not heard, impressions concerning a course to follow were experienced at that time or later which became answers to their prayers."[1]

The temple is a place of peace, refuge, and focus, a place located on earth but not part of the world, a place free of distraction and preoccupation—all prerequisites for the clearest, most powerful revelatory experiences. Just as every advanced course of instruction has prerequisites, so too does revelation. President Boyd K. Packer said:

> When members of the Church are troubled or when crucial decisions weigh heavily upon their minds, it is a common thing for them to go to the temple. It is a good place to take our cares. In the temple we can receive spiritual perspective. There, during the time of the temple service, we are "out of the world."
>
> Sometimes our minds are so beset with problems, and there are so many things clamoring for attention at once that we just cannot think clearly and see clearly. At the temple the dust of distraction seems to settle out, the fog and the haze seem to lift, and we can "see" things that we were not able to see before and find a way through our troubles that we had not previously known.

The Lord will bless us as we attend to the sacred ordinance work of the temples. Blessings there will not be limited to our temple service. We will be blessed in all of our affairs.[2]

The outreach of the temple extends well beyond its walls to affect every aspect of our lives. That is how powerful the temple is.

It has been said that the temple is the Lord's university, and its covenants and ordinances the advanced tutorial on eternity. President Carlos E. Asay, an emeritus member of the Seventy and president of the Salt Lake Temple, once recounted an amusing but instructive incident:

> I attended a stake conference on the University of Utah campus. The speaker who preceded me at the pulpit stated that the BYU was the Lord's University. Then, remembering where he was and realizing that he might be tarred and feathered if he didn't cushion his words, meekly added, "and so is the University of Utah." I stood and corrected the speaker, saying that I respected both the BYU and the U of U but that neither institution was the Lord's University. I stated that the Lord's University was the holy temple. The final speaker, President Gordon B. Hinckley, acknowledged the differences of opinion shared by the other speakers and said, "Let me put the matter to rest—as President Asay has said, 'The Temple is the Lord's University!'" Yes, the temple is the Lord's University. The campus is the sparkling building and its beautiful grounds; the professors are the ordinance workers and the Holy Spirit; the curriculum is the gospel of Jesus Christ; and the instructional approach involves cognitive, affective, and motor or skill learning.

Perfect teaching, like pure religion, involves knowing,

feeling, and doing. It appeals to all of one's senses and results
in an acquisition of knowledge, a stimulation of throbs in the
heart, and actual participation in meaningful activities.[3]

The temple tutors us on who God is and how to act in
his presence—with reverence, solemnity, and consideration
for each other. More than that, the temple shows us how to
become like him whom we are all learning about—God, who
is the reason the temple exists. In the temple we find perfect
instruction.

In fact, President Asay spoke of the temple as the place
of perfect pedagogy. Elder John A. Widtsoe of the Quorum
of the Twelve Apostles described some of his feelings about
the temple as a house of instruction:

> The wonderful pedagogy of the temple service, especially
> appealing to me as a professional teacher, carries with it evi-
> dence of the truth of temple work. We go to the temple to
> be informed and directed to be built up and to be blessed.
> How is all this accomplished? *First* by the spoken word,
> through the lectures and conversation, just as we do in the
> class room, except with more elaborate care; *then* by the
> appeal to the eye by representations by living, moving beings;
> and by pictorial representations in the wonderfully decorated
> rooms. . . . *Meanwhile* the recipients themselves, the candi-
> dates for blessings, engage actively in the temple service. . . .
> Altogether our temple worship follows a most excellent peda-
> gogical system. I wish instruction were given so well in every
> school room throughout the land, for we would then teach
> with more effect than we now do. For these reasons, among
> many others, I've always felt that temple work is a direct evi-
> dence of the truth of the work re-established by the Prophet
> Joseph Smith. It may be that the temple endowment and the

other temple ordinances form the strongest available evidence of the divine inspiration of the Prophet Joseph Smith.[4]

The Lord's university, like the scriptures, uses symbolism to teach participants, although not everything is symbolic. A symbol is something that stands for, or represents, another thing. The word *symbol* is of ancient Greek derivation and means, literally, a "token" or "sign" or "something compared to something else." Perhaps the Lord uses symbols because they can disclose much or little, depending on the experience or maturity of the listener. In that sense, symbols are like parables the Savior used. By using symbols, the Lord has made temple ceremonies, ordinances, and teachings simple enough for beginning temple-goers to appreciate, yet profound enough for prophets to continue learning.

Also, all cultures and peoples use symbols to one degree or another. Symbols are universal and cut across time and space. The Lord used symbols anciently to teach his people. We cannot understand the scriptures without an understanding of the nature of symbols. One of the great gifts parents can give to their children is to teach them about symbols, especially gospel and scriptural symbols. Symbols "are understood by the humble, yet they can excite the intellect of the brightest minds."[5] Symbols require us to think about their intended meanings and the possible applications of those meanings in our lives. We must ponder and pray about the realities that stand behind the symbols. Elder Widtsoe gave valuable counsel:

> No man or woman can come out of the temple endowed as he should be, unless he has seen, beyond the symbol, the mighty realities for which the symbols stand. . . .

To the man or woman who goes through the temple, with open eyes, heeding the symbols and the covenants, and making a steady, continuous effort to understand the full meaning, God speaks His word, and revelations come. The endowment is so richly symbolic that only a fool would attempt to describe it; it is so packed full of revelations to those who exercise their strength to seek and see, that no human words can explain or make clear the possibilities that reside in temple service. The endowment which was given by revelation can best be understood by revelation; and to those who seek most vigorously, with pure hearts, will the revelation be greatest.[6]

The most significant symbols in the temple, as in the gospel, point to Christ in one way or another. Elder Russell M. Nelson has written:

Essential ordinances of the gospel symbolize the Atonement. Baptism by immersion is symbolic of the death, burial, and Resurrection of the Redeemer. Partaking of the sacrament renews baptismal covenants and also renews our memory of the Savior's broken flesh and of the blood He shed for us. Ordinances of the temple symbolize our reconciliation with the Lord and seal families together forever. Obedience to the sacred covenants made in temples qualifies us for eternal life—the greatest gift of God to man—the "object and end of our existence."[7]

The temple is truly the Lord's university. It is a place of perfect teaching because the learning that takes place is tailored to each individual student by the Holy Ghost—one of three perfect, all-powerful Teachers in the universe. President Hinckley said of the temple, "This sacred edifice becomes a school of instruction in the sweet and sacred things of God. Here we have outlined the plan of a loving Father in behalf of His sons and daughters of all generations. Here we have sketched before us the odyssey of man's eternal journey from premortal existence through this life to the life beyond. Great fundamental and basic truths are taught with clarity and simplicity well within the understanding of all who hear."[8]

President Hinckley's equation of the word *temple* with "sacred edifice" is more significant than we might realize at first. The word *edifice* derives from the combination of two Latin terms, *aedis* (literally, "temple") and *facere* ("to make"). *Edifice* is related to *edify* (literally, "to instruct or improve morally or spiritually"). Anciently, the temple was the place where one was instructed and improved morally or spiritually.

To receive the most from our temple experience, as with every course of instruction, it seems reasonable to expect that we go prepared. Part of our preparation involves dressing appropriately to go to the temple. The Lord is not a slouch, and he expects those striving to be like him not to be slouchy—either in their demeanor or their dress. I learned a tremendous lesson from a kindly temple worker the first time I entered the Lord's holy house as a missionary. "Elder, dress like you are going before the Lord." I have never forgotten that experience. It was not a rebuke but a moment of profound insight. It comes forcefully to mind every time I'm in the temple and many times without. I honestly believe great blessings will come from doing even seemingly inconsequential tasks with dignity.

Another prerequisite to receiving the most from the Lord's advanced course is the reverence we possess and exhibit in the temple. Elder L. Lionel Kendrick has provided invaluable insight:

> To be reverent is not just to be quiet. It involves an awareness of what is taking place. It involves a divine desire to learn and to be receptive to the promptings of the Spirit. It involves a striving to seek added light and knowledge. Irreverence is not only an act of disrespect for Deity, but it makes it impossible for the Spirit to teach us the things that we need to know.
>
> It is in the temple that we must speak in reverent tones. Reverence is no minor nor mundane matter. It has eternal consequences and should be treated as divine in nature. To be reverent in the temple, we must sense it to be a place of purity and a place of holiness.[9]

Reverence and learning go together. They are inextricably linked, which is a most significant insight that has come to me. "Reverence involves thinking, speaking, feeling, and acting as we would in the presence of the Lord. . . . Reverence is a supernal form of worship. . . . Our worship in the temple is in preparation to live in the presence of our Heavenly Father and His Son."[10] The temple is not given to us just so we can be *with* God but so we can be *like* God.

We can prepare more fully by striving to leave all worldly thoughts behind upon entering the Lord's university. In addition, our language will be elevated when we leave worldly discussions behind in the world. Again, from Elder Kendrick: "It is inappropriate to discuss matters of business, pleasure, or current events in the temple."[11] I am fairly certain I would try very hard to be sensitive to possible offensive language or behavior when entering the home of an important official or dignitary. Should I be any less sensitive or attentive to such matters in the house of our Master, the Lord Jesus Christ? I can think of no comment that would make me feel worse than the one made by the Savior to David Whitmer: "But your mind has been on the things of the earth more than on the things of me, your Maker, . . . and you have not given heed unto my Spirit. . . . Wherefore, you are left to inquire for yourself" (D&C 30:2–3).

To be left alone by the Lord, left to ourselves, as it were, is a curse far worse than anything mortality can level against us (just reflect on the Savior's experience on the cross). It seems particularly damaging when eternal learning is at stake. How tragic this circumstance would be for any of us to be in, especially since so very much more is available to us in the temple. As President Ezra Taft Benson assured us, "Prayers *are* answered, revelation occurs, and instruction by the Spirit takes place in the holy temples of the Lord."[12] Such is the unimpeachable witness of one who knows.

# 19

## A PLACE OF
## SACRIFICE

*In ancient times, the Lord's temples were places of
sacrifice. They are still places of sacrifice.*

As is taught in the temple, the Lord has always required
his people to offer sacrifice, from the time of our first
parents onward. The type and place of sacrifice have
changed over the ages, but the fundamental principles
undergirding the doctrine of sacrifice have not. Righteous
sacrifices are really symbols of our obedience to the Lord, of
Jesus Christ and his atonement, of our desire to imitate the
Savior and live as he does. Our offering of sacrifice demon-
strates our commitment to follow the Lord above anyone or
anything else.

The word *sacrifice* comes from two Latin words put
together: *sacer* ("sacred") and *facere* ("to make or do"). Thus,
*sacrifice* literally means "to make sacred." When we sacrifice
what the Lord asks, we are making our lives sacred by our
actions—as did the Savior, in whose holy house we are

worshipping when we covenant to offer sacrifices in his name and for his kingdom.

In the period from Adam to Christ, the formal, required sacrifices designated by the Lord were "the firstlings of their flocks" (Moses 5:5). When Adam began to offer the required sacrifices, out of pure obedience rather than complete understanding, an angel of the Lord visited him and instructed him more fully regarding the underlying principle of his offering:

> And after many days an angel of the Lord appeared unto Adam, saying: Why dost thou offer sacrifices unto the Lord? And Adam said unto him: I know not, save the Lord commanded me.
>
> And then the angel spake, saying: This thing is a similitude of the sacrifice of the Only Begotten of the Father, which is full of grace and truth.
>
> Wherefore, thou shalt do all that thou doest in the name of the Son, and thou shalt repent and call upon God in the name of the Son forevermore. (Moses 5:6–8)

Under the ancient sacrificial system, animal sacrifices were symbols of the Atonement, pointing the offerer (and the observers) to the future shedding of Christ's blood in Gethsemane and on the cross. Not only were the animals themselves a type, shadow, and similitude of the bodily sacrifice of Jesus Christ, but they were also a vicarious substitute, a proxy, standing in the stead of the person making the sacrifice (again, a modeling of both the Savior's sacrifice as well as our own proxy service in the temple). The offerer, through the symbolic substitution of an animal, was giving himself wholly to God. The person making the sacrifice was making or declaring his life to be sacred or holy through the offering of a proxy. In later Mosaic times, this transformation was graphically symbolized by the offerer's laying his hands on the living offering, prior to the act of sacrificing, to transfer personal sins and identity to the animal: "And it shall be accepted for [in behalf of] him to make atonement for him" (Leviticus 1:4). Thus, by offering sacrifice according to the will of God, Adam was acting as Jesus Christ would act—who offered sacrifice (himself), according to the will of God (JST Matthew 27:5).

With the coming of Jesus Christ in mortality and the actual shedding of his blood as the "great and last sacrifice" (Alma 34:14), at least two fundamental changes ensued, though sacrifice remained the premier symbol of the Atonement. First, animal sacrifice and the shedding of blood were discontinued, and something else was required as an offering: "Ye shall offer for a sacrifice unto me a broken heart and a contrite spirit," as the resurrected Christ said to the Nephites (3 Nephi 9:20).

Second, an intermediary was no longer required, as in the days of the Mosaic dispensation when the Aaronic priest conducted the actual slaughter of the animal within the tabernacle or temple precincts. Under the new order, every man and woman was empowered to approach God directly and offer his or her own broken heart and contrite spirit.

The symbolism of the Atonement, however, still undergirds the sacrifice. A broken heart and a contrite spirit are a similitude or perfect likeness of Jesus' atoning experience. The word *contrite* comes from a Latin root meaning "to grind." To be contrite is to be "crushed in spirit."[1] In Gethsemane, Jesus' spirit was crushed by the weight of the sins and sorrows of the world (he said he felt "very heavy," or weighed down; Mark 14:33). And on Golgotha's cross, "Jesus died of a broken heart," the consequence of infinite suffering for infinite sin and sorrow.[2]

In the period from Adam to Moses, the designated locations for formal sacrifices were specially constructed altars in various places. In the period from Moses to Christ, the designated locations for formal sacrifice were the specially constructed altars within, first, the Mosaic tabernacle, and, later, Solomon's, Zerubbabel's, and Herod's temples. In our day, the designated locations for making formal covenants of sacrifice are before the sacrament table on the Sabbath and at the altar in the Lord's temples. In the Lord's plan, altars have always been the center of sacred actions. Around the altars in the temples today, the most important and sacred activities occur: the making of covenants, the offering of prayers, the establishment of eternal marriages and families, and the promises of sacrifice and consecration.

The ancient Hebrew language offers some insight into the significance of altars. The word for "sacrifice" is *z*ᵉ*bakh;* the word for "altar" is *mizbeakh,* meaning "(place of) sacrificing." At the altars in the Lord's temples today, worshippers covenant to sacrifice all they possess for the sake of the Lord's kingdom. At the heart of this kind of all-encompassing sacrifice is eternal life, as the *Lectures on Faith* explains:

> Let us here observe, that a religion that does not require the sacrifice of all things never has power sufficient to produce the faith necessary unto life and salvation; for, from the first existence of man, the faith necessary unto the

enjoyment of life and salvation never could be obtained without the sacrifice of all earthly things. It was through this sacrifice, and this only, that God has ordained that men should enjoy eternal life; and it is through the medium of the sacrifice of all earthly things that men do actually know that they are doing the things that are well pleasing in the sight of God. When a man has offered in sacrifice all that he has for the truth's sake, not even withholding his life, and believing before God that he has been called to make this sacrifice because he seeks to do his will, he does know, most assuredly, that God does and will accept his sacrifice and offering, and that he has not, nor will not seek his face in vain. Under these circumstances, then, he can obtain the faith necessary for him to lay hold on eternal life.

It is in vain for persons to fancy to themselves that they are heirs with those, or can be heirs with them, who have offered their all in sacrifice, and by this means obtain faith in God and favor with him so as to obtain eternal life, unless they, in like manner, offer unto him the same sacrifice, and through that offering obtain the knowledge that they are accepted of him.[3]

Thus, the closer we come to God, the more we desire to do what he desires, the more nearly our prayers become "I don't care what I want, Lord; I only care what Thou wants." The nearer we approach God through mighty faith, the more desirous we are to give him everything we possess, everything we *own* and everything we *are*—time, talents, and resources—until we arrive at the point where we will give him the ultimate thing we have to give, the one and only thing that is truly ours (because everything else is already his): our individual agency, our will, our thoughts and desires, as Elder Neal A. Maxwell taught:

> The submission of one's will is really the only uniquely personal thing we have to place on God's altar. The many other things we 'give,' brothers and sisters, are actually the things He has already given or loaned to us. However, when you and I finally submit ourselves, by letting our individual wills be swallowed up in God's will, then we are really giving something to Him! It is the only possession which is truly ours to give!
>
> Consecration thus constitutes the only unconditional surrender which is also a total victory![4]

Here is the great irony of this doctrine (and only in the temple do we get the complete picture): in the giving of everything we have, or may have, to God, we receive everything he has to give to us. That is hardly an even exchange. But that is the sure promise when our hearts and minds are of a celestial order. Then the Lord does not need to ask things of us because he knows we have already given them to him; the carrying out of the sacrifice is a mere formality.

Hence, in the temple we learn that sacrifice is an attitude and not just an action. The covenants of sacrifice we make at the altars in the Lord's temples recall the example of Abraham—whose descendants we are and whose name is spoken with reverence in the temple and in anticipation of a grand reunion with him some day. Abraham was willing to give up everything, including his prized possession—his beloved son Isaac—at the Lord's request (see Genesis 22). And even though he did not carry out the sacrifice of Isaac in physical terms, the sacrifice was already made in

Abraham's mind and heart; only a divine messenger could prevent the patriarch from plunging the knife into his son and letting out his life-blood. In every sense but the physical did Abraham sacrifice Isaac. And God accounted Abraham's faith as though he had indeed taken his son's life.

Abraham's very mindset, his whole-souled outlook, was one of doing the Lord's will, giving the Lord any and all things that He requested. Abraham's life is more than just a fine example of faith; it is the pattern of godly sacrifice, which is taught in the temple. As the Prophet Joseph Smith said, "The sacrifice required of Abraham in the offering up of Isaac, shows that if a man [or woman] would attain to the keys of the kingdom of an endless life[,] he [she] must sacrifice all things."[5] The type of total sacrifice we covenant in the temple to offer is a similitude, a perfect likeness of the Savior's sacrifice. After all, we must be like the Savior in every way, including sacrifice, to be a joint heir with him, as Paul taught: "And if children, then heirs; heirs of God, and joint-heirs with Christ; if so be that we suffer with him, that we may be also glorified together" (Romans 8:17).

The covenant of sacrifice is a "spiritual separator," helping to determine if we are mature enough and capable enough of handling the blessings of exaltation, able to "live in accord with the will of the true and living God or if our hearts are still set 'upon riches and . . . vain things of the world.'"[6] The Lord has put some spiritual separators in place along the way before we can get to the temple. Tithing, for example, is a separator and a schooling process to teach us the principle of consecration and sacrifice and bring us to the point of making temple covenants. If we can't pay our tithing, surely we can't consecrate all we possess and all that we are. It would, in fact, be unfair, unmerciful, of God to allow us into the temple to make promises we are not able to keep.

Temples today are places of sacrifice in various ways. They stand for all the sacrifices that have been made since the beginning of the Restoration to build houses of the Lord. For instance, the kind of sacrifice the Nauvoo Saints offered to construct the first temple in Nauvoo is exemplified in a simple statement from a letter from the Twelve: "Many have volunteered to labor continually."[7]

Temples today stand for the tremendous sacrifices made by Church members who live very far away from a house of the Lord, have few material possessions, and yet give up all they do have just to get to the Lord's house, even if only once in their lives. Many are the stories of such exalting faith in our day.

Temples today reflect the overwhelming yearning that parents have for their children to attend the house of the Lord. Temples stand for all the prayers offered and sacrifices made to help loved ones get to those sacred edifices, where blessings can be secured that will make them truly happy.

I have known such parents and family leaders. The memory of one in particular will always stay with me. This good woman did not possess wealth or influence. She was not well educated or beautiful as the world measures such things. But she was always among the first to volunteer for welfare and cleanup assignments, particularly the unpleasant ones, that used to be given to most wards and branches in the Church from time to time. On one occasion, it was brought to my attention, as her bishop, that she had volunteered again, this time to do some arduous, unpleasant work to help get the newly constructed temple where we lived ready for its open house. I asked to meet with her so I could give her a word of appreciation for all she had done over the years. She deflected my attempt and with great emotion said, "Bishop, I told the Lord I'd scrub floors for the rest of my life if he'd help me raise my boys and get them to the temple. I'm keeping my promise."

I think of righteous men and women whose families were connected to covenants they made in the temple—Hannah, Zacharias and Elisabeth, Joseph and Mary, and the like. And then I think of this good woman who taught me a powerful lesson several years ago, and I am thankful to know that temples are still places of sacrifice.

# 20

## OUR PLACE IN HEAVENLY FATHER'S PLAN

*In the temple we learn about our true identity and our place in our Heavenly Father's plan.*

Because the temple presents the Lord's perspective on time and eternity, we who enter in are able to see more clearly who we really are, why that knowledge is so important, and what we may become. Elder John A. Widtsoe summarized the feelings and powerful promptings we may experience through our worship in the temple:

> The mighty perspective of eternity is unraveled before us in the holy temples; we see time from its infinite beginning to its endless end; and the drama of eternal life is unfolded before us. Then I see more clearly my place amidst the things of the universe, my place among the purposes of God; I am better able to place myself where I belong, and I am better able to value and to weigh, to separate and to organize the common, ordinary duties of my life, so that the little things shall not oppress me or take away my vision of the greater things that God has given us.[1]

191

Knowing our true identity influences our priorities. In truth, we were born to be kings and queens, priests and priestesses, to rule and reign in the house of Israel for eternity through the atonement of Jesus Christ (see Revelation 1:5–6). That is also the testimony of temple teachings.

Our association with the house of Israel began long before we were born into this mortal life. And if we are faithful in mortality, it will continue long after this earth becomes the abode of celestial beings, beings who have been endowed in the house of the Lord (D&C 130:9; 88:17–20). In the words of Elder Melvin J. Ballard, Israel is "a group of souls tested, tried, and proven before they were born into the world. . . . Through this lineage were to come the true and tried souls that had demonstrated their righteousness in the spirit world before they came here."[2]

In the temple we learn that Israel, back through Abraham, is the Lord's foreordained, chosen family, chosen to guard the doctrine and ordinances of eternal increase, chosen to bless all the families of the earth, chosen to be an anchor in a drifting world. This is a chosenness of obligation, not of carefree privilege. Our destiny becomes the destiny of Abraham when we participate in the priesthood ordinances of the temple. We are entitled to the same blessings of Abraham, who "hath entered into his exaltation and sitteth upon his throne" (D&C 132:29). The Lord tells us, "This promise is yours also, because ye are of Abraham" (D&C 132:31). Regardless of original lineage, when we enter the Lord's holy house we are Abraham's seed and "lawful heirs" to his promises and blessings (D&C 86:9; see also 84:34; 86:8–11; 132:31).

In the temple we realize that our potential, our destiny, if we are faithful, is awesome to contemplate. In the New Testament book written to the temple-endowed members of the Church, the Revelation of John, the Lord promises: "Be thou faithful unto death, and I will give thee a crown of life" (Revelation 2:10). And then he says, "Behold, I come quickly; hold that fast [secure] which thou hast, that no man take thy crown. Him that overcometh will I make a pillar in the temple [exalted kingdom] of my God, and he shall go no more out" (Revelation 3:11–12). We will be crowned! Righteous men, as kings and priests, and righteous women, as queens and priestesses, to reign over an endless posterity and receive God's fulness *and* his glory (D&C 76:56; Revelation 1:6). "If the Saints are not to reign," asked the Prophet Joseph Smith, "for what purpose are they crowned?"[3] This is our identity and destiny. We not only hear this taught in the temple but glimpse it as well.

A few years ago, our family met a full-time missionary in our area who was from Mongolia. He taught our son the Mongolian language in preparation for his own mission to Mongolia (no coincidence, I believe). After the missionary's honorable service was completed, he returned to his native Mongolia; he carried with him the fire of the gospel that burned brightly in his eyes. He found a sweetheart, and after many struggles they returned to his mission field to be married in the temple among the members of the Church who had become his gospel family. Many people gathered in the sealing room on the appointed day to witness the exchange of covenants and promises and share in the celebration and joy.

After the sacred words were pronounced by the sealer

and the covenants were made, a great lesson was taught and eternity was glimpsed. The sealer had the couple, dressed all in white, stand in front (and a little to the side) of the mirrors that are specially hung on opposite walls of most sealing rooms. As they looked behind, they saw infinite images of themselves projected in the mirrors as though an eternity's worth of generations stretched backward in time. As they looked forward, they saw infinite images—their images—projected ahead of them. These symbolic "generations," a representation of ancestors and posterity, were linked together through them in the temple. The eternal promises of the priesthood were glimpsed. Past generations and future families converge in the temple as a result of the sealing keys of the priesthood. Neither economic background, ethnicity, culture, levels of education, skin color, or facial features make any difference in the temple. All are destined to become like God, all are destined to rule and reign in the house of Israel, *if* each covenanter remains true and faithful to the covenants made in the Lord's holy home.

Because each individual who is born, or adopted through covenant, into the house of Israel is a king or a queen (upon conditions of faithfulness), no individual will be denied any blessing or privilege because certain opportunities do not present themselves while the person is in mortality. I have in mind those who, for a variety of reasons, have not had the opportunity to be married to a worthy companion and also those couples who have not been blessed with children. The temple is entirely about eternal families and godhood. But our Father in Heaven is *perfectly* fair and *perfectly* loving and, I am certain, will not let any one of his individual children slip through the cracks, so to speak, and be denied the promises of "eternal lives," or eternal increase (D&C 132:24).

You and I were created to be like our Creator, male and female, and no power can take that promise away if we are faithful to Christ's gospel and rely on the merits and mercies of him who is mighty to rescue us in *every* way and powerful enough to bring about the Father's purposes for our lives. In addition, each of us is a child in a family unit and has a tremendous responsibility and work to accomplish, irrespective of our marital status. Each of us is of infinite worth (see D&C 18:10), a truth which the adversary is trying to keep from us. Elder Russell M. Nelson's testimony is a valuable reminder that we are *not* valueless if we have no spouse:

> In a recent statement, President Howard W. Hunter included these remarks: "Let us be a temple-attending and a temple-loving people. Let us hasten to the temple . . . not only for our kindred dead, but let us also go for the personal blessing of temple worship."
>
> President Hunter's invitation reminds us that we can provide names and ordinances for ancestors for whom information is readily available, and, where possible, we can regularly attend the temple. What and how much we do should depend upon personal circumstances and abilities, direction from Church leaders, and guidance from the Spirit. Throughout our lives, each of us can do something significant. . . .
>
> Many travel the highways of life without a companion. They, too, are needed by their families on both sides of the veil. Others may never be able to attend a temple during their mortal lifetime. To the faithful, comfort comes from the knowledge that no blessings will be withheld from any who

love the Lord and strive earnestly to keep His commandments. We will be judged by our deeds *and* the desires of our
hearts—in the Lord's merciful way and time.[4]

Each one of us was born in the time and place we were
born not by chance but according to a divine plan. Paul taught
this very significant doctrine to the Greek philosophers of
his day who were concerned with matters they never would
have understood without the clarifying apostolic voice of
revelation: "And [God] hath made of one blood all nations
of men for to dwell on all the face of the earth, and hath
determined the times before appointed, and the bounds of
their habitation" (Acts 17:26). Mordecai caused Esther to
think about the ennobling truth that we come to earth by
divine design, that our place is known to God: "And who
knoweth whether thou art come to the kingdom for such a
time as this?" (Esther 4:14).

The temple teaches us to appreciate our place in God's
plan by starting with the creation story. Why begin there,
considering that there are other accounts available to us in
Genesis, the book of Moses, and the book of Abraham?
Perhaps because God wants the Saints of each dispensation,
the Saints of each special period of new or reemphasized
doctrines, revelations, and covenants, to know that he
regards them individually. Perhaps he wants them to understand in a personal way their specific and special station in
the eternal scheme of things, in relation to the whole plan.
The account of the creation of this earth becomes a part of
each individual's personal story about his or her place in the
universe and kingdom of God.

Truly, the temple gives to us a sense of our identity. The

temple links *our* time with eternity, showing how and where we fit into both. The temple connects us to generations past and illuminates our future path. The temple helps us to know that we are children of God and the seed of Abraham with a mission, a purpose, an obligation, and a glorious destiny. Temples are like patriarchal blessings. Both chart our course for eternity. Both provide revelation for our place and time. Both experiences are individual and personal. Ultimately, both help us to know we are loved and lovable—and that is part of our identity as well.

# CONCLUSION: PREPARING FOR ETERNITY

Many and great are the blessings of the temple. In the house of the Lord we are given the knowledge and power to receive eternal life. In the temple we may come into the presence of the Lord. In the temple the pure gospel is proclaimed. In the temple the Saints may be perfected. In the temple the dead are redeemed. Service to others is a preparation to receive spiritual manifestations as well as power from on high. In the temple we are brought close to our departed ancestors. "Each new Temple forms an additional bond between the heavens and the earth, marking a new epoch in the mighty work of vicarious redemption by the living for the dead—enabling the Saints to be indeed saviors on Mount Zion."[1]

The greatest responsibility we have been given by God is to seek after our kindred dead. Elder Mark E. Petersen said that "each living person is responsible to assist in the salvation of his own deceased relatives. Our own salvation is largely dependent upon it. . . . [If] we go to the temple, and not for our own dead, we are performing only a part of our duty, because we are also required to go there specifically to save our own dead relatives and bind the various generations together by the power of the holy priesthood."[2]

Temple worship changes our perspective in many ways. We begin to care less about the things of the world and much more about the things of God. President Wilford Woodruff said: "If the veil were lifted off the face of the Latter-day Saints [and they] could see and know the things of God as they do who are laboring for the salvation of the human family who are in the spirit world . . . , this whole people, with very few, if any exceptions, would lose all interest in the riches of the world, and instead thereof *their whole desires and labors would be directed to redeem their dead.*"[3]

The temple invites and fosters personal revelation. In the standard works and pronouncements of modern-day prophets, we find a kind of public revelation. In the temple, as in our personal prayers and yearnings, we receive personal and direct revelation from God himself. The temple stands as a beacon to parents and as an unchanging goal to children. President Ezra Taft Benson elevated our sights when he said:

> The temple is an ever-present reminder that God intends the family to be eternal. How fitting it is for mothers and fathers to point to the temple and say to their children, "That is the place where we were married for eternity." By so doing, the ideal of temple marriage can be instilled within the minds and hearts of your children while they are very young.

I am grateful to the Lord that my temple memories extend back—even to young boyhood. I remember so well, as a little boy, coming in from the field and approaching the old farm house in Whitney, Idaho. I could hear my mother singing "Have I Done Any Good in the World Today?" (*Hymns*, no. 58.)

I can still see her in my mind's eye bending over the ironing board with newspapers on the floor, ironing long strips of white cloth, with beads of perspiration on her forehead. When I asked her what she was doing, she said, "These are temple robes, my son. Your father and I are going to the temple at Logan."

Then she put the old flatiron on the stove, drew a chair close to mine, and told me about temple work—how important it is to be able to go to the temple and participate in the sacred ordinances performed there. She also expressed her fervent hope that some day her children and grandchildren and great-grandchildren would have the opportunity to enjoy these priceless blessings.[4]

It is never too early to teach children the special and sacred nature of the temple. When my family and I lived in Israel, teaching students at the Brigham Young University Center for Near Eastern Studies, we traveled with the students on overnight or week-long field trips to various areas of the country. On more than one occasion we found our youngest daughter, two years of age, after supper in the company of a group of female students, sitting on their laps as they grilled her about two photographs in front of her. One was a picture of the Salt Lake Temple, the other a picture of the Dome of the Rock in Jerusalem. "Where do we go to get married?" they would ask our daughter repeatedly.

Over and over she would point to the temple. I think it became a competition among the different groups to see who could be the first to get our two year old to say the words "in the temple." No one in our family has forgotten that experience, and today there is no question in the mind of our youngest child about the importance of the temple.

The temple builds, strengthens, guides, and protects marriages and families. President Joseph Fielding Smith taught that a tremendous advantage comes to those whose parents are sealed by the authority of the holy priesthood. "Being *heirs* they have claims on the blessings of the gospel beyond what those not so born are entitled to receive. They may receive a greater guidance, a greater protection, a greater inspiration from the Spirit of the Lord."[5]

The sealing ordinances performed in temples result in eternal consequences that we cannot presently fully comprehend or appreciate with our limited mortal perspective. In speaking of the lasting effects of the sealing ordinance ratified by the Holy Ghost (see D&C 132:7), the Prophet Joseph Smith said, "When a seal is put upon the father and mother, it secures their posterity, so that they cannot be lost, but will be saved by virtue of the covenant of their father and mother."[6] Of course there are different degrees of salvation, but the point is that no child sealed to righteous parents will ever be lost. That is the message presented by Elder Orson F. Whitney as well:

> You parents of the wilful and the wayward! Don't give them up. Don't cast them off. They are not utterly lost. The Shepherd will find his sheep. They were his before they were yours—long before he entrusted them to your care; and you

cannot begin to love them as he loves them. . . . Our Heavenly Father is far more merciful, infinitely more charitable, than even the best of his servants, and the Everlasting Gospel is mightier in power to save than our narrow finite minds can comprehend.

The Prophet Joseph Smith declared—and he never taught more comforting doctrine—that the eternal sealings of faithful parents and the divine promises made to them for valiant service in the Cause of Truth, would save not only themselves, but likewise their posterity. Though some of the sheep may wander, the eye of the Shepherd is upon them, and sooner or later they will feel the tentacles of Divine Providence reaching out after them and drawing them back to the fold. Either in this life or in the life to come, they will return. They will have to pay their debt to justice; they will suffer for their sins; and may tread a thorny path; but if it leads them at last, like the penitent Prodigal, to a loving and forgiving father's heart and home, the painful experience will not have been in vain. Pray for your careless and disobedient children; hold on to them with your faith. Hope on, trust on, till you see the salvation of God.

Who are these straying sheep—these wayward sons and daughters? They are the children of the Covenant, heirs to the promises, and have received, if baptized, the gift of the Holy Ghost, which makes manifest the things of God. Could all that go for naught?[7]

Elder Boyd K. Packer also spoke about the power of the sealing ordinances to bind parents and children to each other in a world that seems, at times, set on destroying families. In a general conference address in April 1992, he said:

It is a great challenge to raise a family in the darkening mists of our moral environment.

We emphasize that the greatest work you will do will be within the walls of your home (see Harold B. Lee, *Ensign*, July 1973, p. 98), and that 'no other success can compensate for failure in the home' (David O. McKay, *Improvement Era*, June 1964, p. 445). . . .

It is not uncommon for responsible parents to lose one of their children, for a time, to influences over which they have no control. They agonize over rebellious sons or daughters. They are puzzled over why they are so helpless when they have tried so hard to do what they should.

It is my conviction that those wicked influences one day will be overruled. . . .

We cannot overemphasize the value of temple marriage, the binding ties of the sealing ordinance, and the standards of worthiness required of them. When parents keep the covenants they have made at the altar of the temple, their children will be forever bound to them.[8]

The temple is also a place of healing; it is the receptacle of the Balm of Gilead. In ancient times, a region in the Holy Land called Gilead was noted for its balm, an aromatic resin or salve that when applied to wounds or afflictions relieved pain, soothed, and healed.

The temple is truly many things:

- the home of the Lord
- the Lord's university
- a place of peace
- a place of hope
- a place of covenant
- a place of blessing

- a place of godliness
- a place of visitation
- a place of healing

President Benson has promised us that when we attend the temple in worthiness and perform the ordinances of the house of the Lord, great blessings will come to us.[9] We will—

- receive the spirit of Elijah, which will turn our hearts to our spouses, to our children, and to our ancestors
- love our families with a deeper love than we ever have before
- be endowed with power from on high, just as the Lord promised in the Doctrine and Covenants (38:32; 95:8)
- receive the key of the knowledge of God (see D&C 84:19)
- learn how we can be like God
- receive the power of godliness

The world is bad and getting worse. Soon it may be that the only sure refuge will be found in three holy places, and three only: in the Lord's temples, in the stakes of Zion, and in our homes. Those places are three pillars of the celestial kingdom. In each, the will of the Lord can be manifested to us. May we go often to the temple and, in the going, strengthen our homes and make them a heaven and a haven on earth. As our beloved President Howard W. Hunter said, "May you let the meaning and beauty and peace of the temple come into your everyday life more directly in order that the millennial day may come, that promised time when 'they shall beat their swords into plowshares, and their spears into pruninghooks: nation shall not lift up sword against nation, neither shall they learn war any more . . . [but shall] walk in the light of the Lord' (Isaiah 2:4–5)."[10] President Hunter's eye was firmly fixed on the Lord's holy house. May ours be so fixed, as well. And may our temple worship lay the foundation for the magnificent millennial day and beyond. Truly, temple worship is a unique symbol of our commitment to Jesus Christ and our membership in the kingdom of God.

# NOTES

**Introduction: Reflections on the Temple**

1. See Nibley, *Temple and Cosmos*, 1–41.
2. Nibley, *Temple and Cosmos*, 15, 25, 83.
3. See Skinner, "Ancient People of Qumran," 13.
4. Yadin, *Temple Scroll*, 113.
5. Romney, "The Gates to Heaven," *Ensign*, March 1971, 16.
6. Asay, "Temple Blessings and Applications," 1.

**Chapter 1. The Ultimate Expression of Our Worship**

1. Hinckley, "Of Missions, Temples, and Stewardship," *Ensign*, November 1995, 53.
2. Nelson, "The Exodus Repeated," *Ensign*, July 1999, 10.
3. Fielding, as quoted in Ehat, "'They Might Have Known That He Was Not a Fallen Prophet,'" *BYU Studies* 19, no. 2 (1979): 158.
4. Smith, *History of the Church*, 7:567.
5. Smith, *History of the Church*, 7:579.
6. As quoted in Brown, "Sacred Departments for Temple Work in Nauvoo," *BYU Studies* 19, no. 3 (1979): 374.
7. Nelson, "Prepare for Blessings of the Temple," *Ensign*, March 2002, 22.
8. Packer, "The Holy Temple," *Ensign*, February 1995, 32.
9. *Brigham Young*, 58; emphasis added.
10. Smith, *History of the Church*, 6:230.

## Chapter 2. The Promise of Eternal Life

1. First Presidency, "The Origin of Man"; reprinted in *Ensign*, February 2002, 29.
2. Smith, *Teachings of the Prophet Joseph Smith*, 345–46; see also 342–62.
3. Smith, *Lectures on Faith*, 3.24.
4. Hinckley, "The Father, Son, and Holy Ghost," *Ensign*, November 1986, 49.
5. Smith, *Teachings of the Prophet Joseph Smith*, 347.

## Chapter 3. Ordinances and Covenants

1. Smith, *Teachings of the Prophet Joseph Smith*, 354.
2. Smith, *Teachings of the Prophet Joseph Smith*, 220; emphasis added.
3. Smith, *Teachings of the Prophet Joseph Smith*, 324.
4. *Brigham Young*, 67.
5. Taylor, *Journal of Discourses*, 21:95.
6. McConkie, *Mormon Doctrine*, 781.

## Chapter 4. Essential Ordinances of Salvation

1. Smith, *Teachings of the Prophet Joseph Smith*, 219.
2. Hunter, "All Are Alike unto God," *Ensign*, June 1979, 72.
3. Hunter, "All Are Alike unto God," *Ensign*, June 1979, 72.
4. Smith, *Teachings of the Prophet Joseph Smith*, 308–9; emphasis added.
5. Smith, *Teachings of the Prophet Joseph Smith*, 363; emphasis added.
6. Smith, *Teachings of the Prophet Joseph Smith*, 331; emphasis added.
7. Faust, "Eternity Lies Before Us," *Ensign*, May 1997, 20.
8. Widtsoe, "Looking toward the Temple," *Improvement Era*, October 1962, 710.
9. Nelson, "Prepare for Blessings of the Temple," *Ensign*, March 2002, 19–20.

## Chapter 5. Priesthood Power and Priesthood Organization

1. Smith, *Teachings of the Prophet Joseph Smith*, 157–58.
2. Smith, Conference Report, October 1966, 84.
3. Smith, *Teachings of the Prophet Joseph Smith*, 181.
4. Smith, *Teachings of the Prophet Joseph Smith*, 157–58.
5. Benson, "What I Hope You Will Teach Your Children about the Temple," *Ensign*, August 1985, 8.
6. Smith, *Doctrines of Salvation*, 3:126–27.
7. Smith, *Doctrines of Salvation*, 3:133; emphasis added.
8. Benson, "What I Hope You Will Teach Your Children about the Temple," *Ensign*, August 1985, 9–10.

9. Smith, *Teachings of the Prophet Joseph Smith*, 158.
10. Smith, *Teachings of the Prophet Joseph Smith*, 157.
11. Smith, *Teachings of the Prophet Joseph Smith*, 157.
12. Smith, *Teachings of the Prophet Joseph Smith*, 224.
13. Gordon B. Hinckley, quoted in Asay, "Temple Blessings and Applications," 11.
14. Benson, "What I Hope You Will Teach Your Children about the Temple," *Ensign*, August 1985, 10.
15. See Packer, "The Holy Temple," *Ensign*, February 1995, 36.

## Chapter 6. The Atonement of Jesus Christ

1. Smith, *Teachings of the Prophet Joseph Smith*, 121.
2. Nelson, "Prepare for the Blessings of the Temple," *Ensign*, March 2002, 22.
3. *Times and Seasons* 4 (1 February 1843): 82–83.
4. Smith, *Teachings of the Prophet Joseph Smith*, 181.
5. Smith, *Teachings of the Prophet Joseph Smith*, 189.
6. Pratt, *The Seer* 1, no. 4, 54 (punctuation standardized).
7. Haight, "Personal Temple Worship," *Ensign*, May 1993, 25.
8. Haight, "Personal Temple Worship," *Ensign*, May 1993, 25
9. Christofferson, "The Redemption of the Dead," *Ensign*, Nov. 2000, 9–10.
10. Christofferson, "The Redemption of the Dead," *Ensign*, Nov. 2000, 10.

## Chapter 7. The Richest Gifts on Earth

1. Smith, *Teachings of the Prophet Joseph Smith*, 91.
2. Quoted in Asay, "Temple Blessings and Applications," 4.
3. Quoted in Ehat, "Who Shall Ascend to the Hill of the Lord," in Parry, *Temples of the Ancient World*, 58.
4. Asay, "Temple Blessings and Applications," 4.
5. Young, *Journal of Discourses*, 2:31.
6. Talmage, *House of the Lord*, 99.
7. Quoted in Ehat, "Who Shall Ascend to the Hill of the Lord," in Parry, *Temples of the Ancient World*, 58.
8. Packer, *Holy Temple*, 153.
9. Nibley, "Meanings and Functions of Temples," in *Encyclopedia of Mormonism*, 4:1461.
10. Nibley, "Meanings and Functions of Temples," in *Encyclopedia of Mormonism*, 4:1461.
11. In Charlesworth, *Old Testament Pseudepigrapha*, 1:137, 139.

12. Charlesworth, *Old Testament Pseudepigrapha*, 1:750.
13. Nibley, *Temple and Cosmos*, 122. See also *Gospel of Truth* 23:33; 24:7, in Robinson, *Nag Hammadi Library in English*, 41.
14. Nibley, *Message of the Joseph Smith Papyri*, 445.
15. Nibley, *Message of the Joseph Smith Papyri*, 445.
16. Asay, "Temple Blessings and Applications," 5.
17. Asay, "Temple Blessings and Applications," 6.

### Chapter 8. The Sealing Ordinances

1. Packer, "The Holy Temple," *Ensign*, February 1995, 34.
2. McConkie, *Mormon Doctrine*, 683.
3. Smith, *Doctrines of Salvation*, 2:111–12.
4. Smith, *Teachings of the Prophet Joseph Smith*, 337.
5. Smith, *Teachings of the Prophet Joseph Smith*, 157.
6. Packer, *Holy Temple*, 83–84.
7. Smith, *Doctrines of Salvation*, 2:117.
8. Talmage, *Articles of Faith*, 145–46.
9. Smith, *Teachings of the Prophet Joseph Smith*, 149–50.
10. McConkie, *Mormon Doctrine*, 683.
11. McConkie, *Mormon Doctrine*, 683.
12. Smith, *Doctrines of Salvation*, 2:46.
13. Smith, *Teachings of the Prophet Joseph Smith*, 150.
14. Smith, *Teachings of the Prophet Joseph Smith*, 149–51.

### Chapter 9. Becoming like Our Father in Heaven

1. Smith, *Doctrines of Salvation*, 2:44.
2. Smith, *Doctrines of Salvation*, 2:48.
3. Smith, *Doctrines of Salvation*, 2:35.
4. Smith, *Teachings of the Prophet Joseph Smith*, 346–47.
5. Smith, *Teachings of the Prophet Joseph Smith*, 345.
6. Smith, *Teachings of the Prophet Joseph Smith*, 369–71, 373.
7. Snow, "Devotion to a Divine Inspiration," *Improvement Era*, June 1919, 656.
8. Clendenin, *Eastern Orthodox Christianity*, 126.
9. Clendenin, *Eastern Orthodox Christianity*, 127.
10. Irenaeus, *Against Heresies* 5, preface, quoted in Clendenin, *Eastern Orthodox Christianity*, 127.
11. Clement of Alexandria, *Exhortation to the Gentiles* 1, quoted in Robinson, *Are Mormons Christians?* 61.
12. Justin Martyr, *Dialogue with Trypho*, 124, quoted in Robinson, *Are Mormons Christians?* 61.

13. Quoted in Clendenin, *Eastern Orthodox Christianity,* 127.
14. Athanasius, *Against the Arians* 1.39; 3.34, quoted in Robinson, *Are Mormons Christians?* 61.
15. Augustine, *On the Psalms,* 50:2, quoted in Robinson, *Are Mormons Christians?* 61.
16. Lewis, *Weight of Glory and Other Addresses,* 39.
17. Lewis, *Mere Christianity,* 154.
18. Lewis, *Mere Christianity,* 155.
19. Lewis, *Mere Christianity,* 176.

## Chapter 10. Establishing and Nurturing Eternal Families

1. Packer, "Little Children," *Ensign,* November 1986, 16.
2. Faust, "Challenges Facing the Family," Worldwide Leadership Training Meeting, January 10, 2004, 1–2.
3. Hinckley, "Standing Strong and Immovable," Worldwide Leadership Training Meeting, January 10, 2004, 20.
4. Smith, *Teachings of the Prophet Joseph Smith,* 323.
5. Smith, *History of the Church,* 4:366.
6. Smith, *Teachings of the Prophet Joseph Smith,* 308.
7. Smith, *History of the Church,* 4:492–93.
8. See Article of Faith 10.
9. Smith, *Teachings of the Prophet Joseph Smith,* 309.
10. Snow, *Teachings of Lorenzo Snow,* 137–38.
11. Smith, *Teachings of the Prophet Joseph Smith,* 300–301.
12. Smith, *Doctrines of Salvation,* 2:65.
13. Smith, *Doctrines of Salvation,* 2:66–67.

## Chapter 11. Adam and Eve Received the Sealing Ordinances

1. Smith, *Teachings of the Prophet Joseph Smith,* 308.
2. Smith, *Teachings of the Prophet Joseph Smith,* 59–60.
3. Smith, *Teachings of the Prophet Joseph Smith,* 308.
4. McConkie, *Mormon Doctrine,* 16–17.
5. McConkie, *Mormon Doctrine,* 242.
6. Benson, "What I Hope You Will Teach Your Children about the Temple," *Ensign,* August 1985, 8.
7 Quoted in Smith, *Doctrines of Salvation,* 2:70.
8. Smith, *Doctrines of Salvation,* 2:70.
9. Smith, *Doctrines of Salvation,* 2:70.
10. Smith, *Doctrines of Salvation,* 2:71.
11. Smith, *Doctrines of Salvation,* 2:67–68.
12. Smith, *Doctrines of Salvation,* 2:24.

## Chapter 12. Temple Ordinances in Earlier Dispensations

1. Smith, *Teachings of the Prophet Joseph Smith*, 170.
2. Romney, "Temples—The Gates to Heaven," *Ensign*, March 1971, 16.
3. McConkie, "The Doctrinal Restoration," in Nyman and Millet, *Joseph Smith Translation*, 19–20.
4. Smith, *Teachings of the Prophet Joseph Smith*, 181.
5. McConkie, *Mormon Doctrine*, 805.
6. See Taylor, *Journal of Discourses*, 20:174–75; 21:65, 94.
7. Kimball, *Journal of Discourses*, 10:241.
8. Smith, *Doctrines of Salvation*, 2:165; McConkie, *Doctrinal New Testament Commentary*, 1:400.
9. Ehat and Cook, *Words of Joseph Smith*, Ehat and Cook, 211.
10. Eusebius, *Ecclesiastical History*, 2:1:4.
11. Eusebius, *Ecclesiastical History*, 1:13:20.
12. Nibley, *Temple and Cosmos*, 121.
13. Nibley, *Temple and Cosmos*, 121–22.
14. Nibley, *Temple and Cosmos*, 122.
15. Quoted in Nibley, *Temple and Cosmos*, 119.
16. Haight, "Personal Temple Worship," *Ensign*, May 1993, 24.

## Chapter 13. Gathering the Saints for the Building of Temples

1. Smith, *Teachings of the Prophet Joseph Smith*, 307–8.
2. Smith, *Teachings of the Prophet Joseph Smith*, 308.
3. Wordsworth, *Ode: Intimations on Immortality from Recollections of Early Childhood*, lines 59–66.
4. Young, *Journal of Discourses*, 2:32.
5. Josephus, *Wars of the Jews* 6.10.1., 588.
6. Smith, *Teachings of the Prophet Joseph Smith*, 322–23; emphasis added.
7. Smith, *Church History and Modern Revelation*, 2:268, quoted in *Doctrine and Covenants Student Manual*, 307.
8. Young, *Discourses of Brigham Young*, 394.
9. Smith, *Doctrines of Salvation*, 2:251–52.

## Chapter 14. A Protection for the Saints

1. Monson, "The Temple of the Lord," *Ensign*, May 1993, 5.
2. Neuenschwander, "Holy Place, Sacred Space," *Ensign*, May 2003, 72.
3. Haight, "Personal Temple Worship," *Ensign*, May 1993, 23.
4. *Millennial Star*, 12 November 1877, 743; quoted in Packer, "The Holy Temple," *Ensign*, February 1995, 36.
5. Hunter, "A Temple-Motivated People," *Ensign*, February 1995, 3.
6. Smith, *Doctrines of Salvation*, 2:252–53.

7. Asay, "The Temple Garment," *Ensign*, August 1997, 19.

8. Asay, "The Temple Garment," *Ensign*, August 1997, 19, 20, 21.

9. Quoted in Staheli, "Obedience—Life's Great Challenge," *Ensign*, May 1998, 82.

10. Packer, "The Holy Temple," *Ensign*, February 1995, 36.

11. Holland, "What I Wish Every New Member Knew—and Every Longtime Member Remembered," *Ensign*, October 2006, 13.

## Chapter 15. Sealing Families Back to Our First Parents

1. Nelson, "Prepare for Blessings of the Temple," *Ensign*, March 2002, 17–18.

2. Kimball, "The Things of Eternity—Stand We in Jeopardy?" *Ensign*, January 1977, 3.

3. Smith, *Teachings of the Prophet Joseph Smith*, 193.

4. Smith, *Teachings of the Prophet Joseph Smith*, 191.

5. Smith, *Teachings of the Prophet Joseph Smith*, 330.

6. Young, *Discourses of Brigham Young*, 407; or *Brigham Young*, 310.

7. Young, *Discourses of Brigham Young*, 406.

8. Young, *Discourses of Brigham Young*, 407.

9. Young, *Discourses of Brigham Young*, 409–410.

10. David B. Galbraith, e-mail, October 13, 1999.

11. Bennett, *Improvement Era*, Oct. 1952, 720.

12. Kimball, "The Things of Eternity," 3.

13. Sanders, *What About Those Who Have Never Heard?* 7.

14. Sanders, *What About Those Who Have Never Heard?* 7.

15. Sanders, *What About Those Who Have Never Heard?* 9.

16. Ronald H. Nash, quoted in Sanders, *What About Those Who Have Never Heard?* 130.

17. Smith, *Teachings of the Prophet Joseph Smith*, 121.

18. Smith, *Teachings of the Prophet Joseph Smith*, 356.

19. Haight, "Personal Temple Worship," *Ensign*, May 1993, 25.

## Chapter 16. Worthiness to Enter the House of the Lord

1. Nelson, "Prepare for Blessings of the Temple," *Ensign*, March 2002, 17.

2. Lyon, Gundry, and Parry, *Best Loved Stories of the LDS People*, 239–40.

3. Nelson, "Prepare for Blessings of the Temple," *Ensign*, March 2002, 19.

## Chapter 17. A Portal to Heaven

1. Letter of Oliver Cowdery to John F. Boynton, 6 May 1834, Oliver Cowdery Letter Book, 45–46, in Anderson and Faulring, *Documentary History of Oliver Cowdery*, 2:150–51.

2. Backman, *Heavens Resound*, 285.

3. Smith, *History of the Church*, 2:379–80.

4. Smith, *History of the Church*, 2:381–82.

5. Smith, *History of the Church*, 2:287.

6. Young, *Journal of Discourses*, 2:31.

7. Snow, *Journal of Erastus Snow*, 5–6.

8. Smith, *History of the Church*, 2:427.

9. Smith, *History of the Church*, 2:427.

10. Smith, *History of the Church*, 2:428.

11. *Testimonies for the Truth*, 10–11.

12. Whitney, *Life of Heber C. Kimball*, 93.

13. Woodruff, *Journal of Discourses*, 19:229.

14. Woodruff, Conference Report, April 1898, 89–90.

15. Quoted in Anderson, *The Other Eminent Men of Wilford Woodruff*, 420.

16. Hinckley, quoted in *Church News*, June 29, 2002, 6.

17. Hinckley, quoted in *Church News*, June 29, 2002, 4; emphasis added.

18. Hinckley, quoted in *Church News*, June 29, 2002, 4; emphasis added.

19. Quoted in Walker, *Diary of Charles Lowell Walker*, 2:509.

**Chapter 18. A Place of Personal Revelation and Education**

1. Hinckley, "The Salt Lake Temple," *Ensign*, March 1993, 6.

2. Packer, "The Holy Temple," *Ensign*, February 1995, 36.

3. Asay, "Temple Blessings and Applications," 3.

4. Quoted in Asay, "Temple Blessings and Applications," 3.

5. Nelson, "Prepare for Blessings of the Temple," *Ensign*, March 2002, 21.

6. Widtsoe, "Symbolism in the Temples," quoted in "Why Symbols?" *Ensign*, February 2007, 15.

7. Nelson, "The Atonement," *Ensign*, November 1996, 35.

8. Hinckley, "The Salt Lake Temple," *Ensign*, March 1993, 5–6.

9. Kendrick, "Enhancing Our Temple Experience," *Ensign*, May 2001, 78.

10. Kendrick, "Enhancing Our Temple Experience," *Ensign*, May 2001, 78–79.

11. Kendrick, "Enhancing Our Temple Experience," *Ensign*, May 2001, 79.

12. Benson, "'Come unto Christ, and Be Perfected in Him,'" *Ensign*, May 1988, 85; emphasis added.

## Chapter 19. A Place of Sacrifice

1. *Webster's New World Dictionary*, s.v. "Contrite."
2. Talmage, *Jesus the Christ*, 669.
3. Smith, *Lectures on Faith*, 6.7–8.
4. Maxwell, "'Swallowed Up in the Will of the Father,'" *Ensign*, November 1995, 24.
5. Smith, *Teachings of the Prophet Joseph Smith*, 322.
6. Nelson, "Personal Preparation for Temple Blessings," *Ensign*, May 2001, 33.
7. Smith, *History of the Church*, 4:434.

## Chapter 20. Our Place in Heavenly Father's Plan

1. Widtsoe, Conference Report, April 1922, 97-98; quoted in Hunter, "The Great Symbol of Our Membership," *Ensign*, October 1994, 2-3.
2. Ballard, *Melvin J. Ballard*, 218–19.
3. Smith, *History of the Church*, 2:20.
4. Nelson, "The Spirit of Elijah," *Ensign*, November 1994, 86.

## Conclusion: Preparing for Eternity

1. Clark, *Messages of the First Presidency*, 5:256.
2. Petersen, "The Message of Elijah," *Ensign*, May 1976, 15–16.
3. Woodruff, *Discourses of Wilford Woodruff*, 152; emphasis added.
4. Benson, "What I Hope You Will Teach Your Children about the Temple," *Ensign*, August 1985, 6, 8.
5. Smith, *Doctrines of Salvation*, 2:90.
6. Smith, *Teachings of the Prophet Joseph Smith*, 321.
7. Whitney, Conference Report, April 1929, 110–11.
8. Packer, "Our Moral Environment," *Ensign*, May, 1992, 66–67.
9. Benson, "What I Hope You Will Teach Your Children about the Temple," *Ensign*, August 1985, 10.
10. Hunter, "Follow the Son of God," *Ensign*, November 1994, 88.

# SOURCES

Anderson, Richard Lloyd, and Scott H. Faulring, eds. *The Documentary History of Oliver Cowdery*. 2 vols. Provo, Utah: Foundation for Ancient Research and Mormon Studies, 1999.

Anderson, Vicki Jo. *The Other Eminent Men of Wilford Woodruff*. Malta, Ida.: Nelson Book, 2000.

Asay, Carlos E. "Temple Blessings and Applications." 1998. Unpublished manuscript in author's possession.

———. "The Temple Garment: 'An Outward Expression of an Inward Commitment.'" *Ensign*, August 1997, 19.

Backman, Milton V., Jr., *The Heavens Resound*. Salt Lake City: Deseret Book, 1983.

Ballard, Melvin J. *Melvin J. Ballard: Crusader for Righteousness*. Salt Lake City: Bookcraft, 1966.

Benson, Ezra Taft. "What I Hope You Will Teach Your Children about the Temple." *Ensign*, August 1985, 6.

———. "'Come unto Christ, and Be Perfected in Him.'" *Ensign*. May 1988, 84.

*Brigham Young*. A volume in *Teachings of Presidents of the Church* series. Salt Lake City: The Church of Jesus Christ of Latter-day Saints, 1997.

Brown, Lisle G. "The Sacred Departments for Temple Work in Nauvoo: The Assembly Room and the Council Chamber." *BYU Studies* 19, no. 3 (1979): 374.

SOURCES

Charlesworth, James H., ed. *Old Testament Pseudepigrapha.* 2 vols. Garden City, N.Y.: Doubleday, 1983, 1985.

Christofferson, D. Todd. "The Redemption of the Dead and the Testimony of Jesus." *Ensign.* November 2000, 9.

Clark, James R. *Messages of the First Presidency 1833–1964.* 6 vols. Salt Lake City: Bookcraft, 1965–75.

Clendenin, Daniel B. *Eastern Orthodox Christianity.* 2d ed. Grand Rapids, Mich.: Baker Academic, 2003.

*Doctrine and Covenants Student Manual.* Prepared by the Church Educational System. Salt Lake City: The Church of Jesus Christ of Latter-day Saints, 2001.

Ehat, Andrew F. "'They Might Have Known That He Was Not a Fallen Prophet': The Nauvoo Journal of Joseph Fielding." *BYU Studies* 19, no. 2, 1979.

Ehat, Andrew F., and Lyndon W. Cook, comps. and eds. *Words of Joseph Smith,* Andrew F. Ehat and Lyndon W. Cook. Orem, Utah: Grandin Book, 1991.

Faust, James E. "Challenges Facing the Family." Worldwide Leadership Training Meeting, January 10, 2004.

———. "Eternity Lies Before Us." *Ensign,* May 1997, 18.

First Presidency [Joseph F. Smith, John R. Winder, and Anthon H. Lund]. "The Origin of Man." *Improvement Era,* November 1909, 75–81. Reprinted in "Gospel Classics: The Origin of Man," *Ensign,* February 2002, 26.

Haight, David B. "Personal Temple Worship." *Ensign,* May 1993, 23.

Hinckley, Gordon B. "The Father, Son, and Holy Ghost," *Ensign,* November 1986, 49.

———. "The Salt Lake Temple." *Ensign,* March 1993, 2.

———. "Standing Strong and Immovable." Worldwide Leadership Training Meeting, January 10, 2004.

Holland, Jeffrey R. "What I Wish Every New Member Knew—and Every Longtime Member Remembered." *Ensign,* October 2006, 10.

Hunter, Howard W. "A Temple-Motivated People." *Ensign,* February 1995, 2.

———. "All Are Alike unto God." *Ensign,* June 1979, 72.

———. "Follow the Son of God." *Ensign,* November 1994, 87.

———. "The Great Symbol of Our Membership," *Ensign,* October 1994, 2.

Josephus, *Wars of the Jews.* In *Josephus Complete Works,* William Whiston, trans. Grand Rapids, MI: Kregel Publications, 1973.

*Journal of Discourses.* 26 vols. London: Latter-day Saints' Book Depot, 1854–86.

Kimball, Spencer W. "The Things of Eternity—Stand We in Jeopardy?" *Ensign*, January 1977, 3.

Lewis, C. S. *Mere Christianity*. New York: Touchstone, 1996.

———. *The Weight of Glory and Other Addresses*. New York: Touchstone, 1996.

Ludlow, Daniel H., ed. *Encyclopedia of Mormonism*. 4 vols. New York: Macmillan, 1992.

Lyon, Jack M., Linda Ririe Gundry, and Jay A. Parry, eds. *Best Loved Stories of the LDS People*. Salt Lake City: Deseret Book, 1992.

Maxwell, Neal A. "'Swallowed Up in the Will of the Father.'" *Ensign*, November 1995, 22.

McConkie, Bruce R. *Doctrinal New Testament Commentary*. 3 vols. Salt Lake City: Bookcraft, 1965–73.

———. "The Doctrinal Restoration." In *The Joseph Smith Translation*. Ed. Monte S. Nyman and Robert L. Millet. Provo: Brigham Young University, 1985.

———. *Mormon Doctrine*. 2d ed. Salt Lake City: Bookcraft, 1979.

Monson, Thomas S. "The Temple of the Lord." *Ensign*, May 1993, 4.

Nelson, Russell M. "The Exodus Repeated." *Ensign*, July 1999, 7.

———. "Personal Preparation for Temple Blessings." *Ensign*, May 2001, 32.

———. "Prepare for Blessings of the Temple." *Ensign*, March 2002, 17.

———. "The Spirit of Elijah." *Ensign*, November 1994, 84.

Neuenschwander, Dennis B. "Holy Place, Sacred Space." *Ensign*, May 2003, 71.

Nibley, Hugh W. *The Message of the Joseph Smith Papyri*. 2d ed. Salt Lake City: Deseret Book, 2005.

———. *Temple and Cosmos*. Ed. Don E. Norton. Salt Lake City: Deseret Book and FARMS, 1992.

Nyman, Monte S., and Robert L. Millet, eds. *The Joseph Smith Translation*. Provo: Brigham Young University, 1985.

Packer, Boyd K. "The Holy Temple." *Ensign*, February 1995, 32.

———. *The Holy Temple*. Salt Lake City: Bookcraft, 1980.

———. "Little Children." *Ensign*, November 1986, 16.

Parry, Donald W., ed. *Temples of the Ancient World*. Salt Lake City: Deseret Book, 1994.

Parry, Donald, and Dana Pike, eds. *LDS Perspectives on the Dead Sea Scrolls*. Provo: FARMS, 1997.

Petersen, Mark E. "The Message of Elijah." *Ensign*, May 1976, 14.

Pratt, Orson. *The Seer*. Vol. 1, No. 4.

Robinson, James. *Nag Hammadi Library in English*. San Francisco: HarperCollins, 1990.

Robinson, Stephen. *Are Mormons Christians?* Salt Lake City: Bookcraft, 1991.

Romney, Marion G. "Temples—The Gates to Heaven." *Ensign*, March 1971, 12.

Sanders, John, ed. *What About Those Who Have Never Heard?* Downers Grove, Ill: InterVarsity Press, 1995.

Skinner, Andrew C. "The Ancient People of Qumran: An Introduction to the Dead Sea Scrolls." In Donald Parry and Dana Pike, eds. *LDS Perspectives on the Dead Sea Scrolls.* Provo: FARMS, 1997.

Smith, Joseph. *Lectures on Faith.* Salt Lake City: Deseret Book, 1985.

Smith, Joseph. *History of the Church.* 7 vols. B. H. Roberts, ed. Salt Lake City: Deseret Book, 1980.

Smith, Joseph. *Teachings of the Prophet Joseph Smith.* Sel. Joseph Fielding Smith. American Fork, Utah: Covenant Communications, 2002.

Smith, Joseph Fielding. *Doctrines of Salvation.* Compiled by Bruce R. McConkie. 3 vols. Salt Lake City: Bookcraft, 1954–56.

Snow, LeRoi C. "Devotion to a Divine Inspiration." *Improvement Era,* June 1919.

Snow, Lorenzo. *The Teachings of Lorenzo Snow.* Comp. Clyde J. Williams. Salt Lake City: Bookcraft, 1984.

Staheli, Donald L. "Obedience—Life's Great Challenge." *Ensign,* May 1998, 81.

Talmage, James E. *Articles of Faith.* Salt Lake City: Deseret Book, 1984.

———. *The House of the Lord.* Salt Lake City: Deseret Book, 1976.

———. *Jesus the Christ.* American Fork, Utah: Covenant Communications, 2002.

*Testimonies for the Truth: A Record of Manifestations.* Liverpool, England, 1853.

Walker, Charles L. *Diary of Charles L. Walker.* 2 vols. Ed. A. Karl Larson and Katharine Miles Larson. Logan, Utah: Utah State University Press, 1980.

Whitney, Orson F. *Life of Heber C. Kimball.* Salt Lake City: Stevens and Wallis, 1945.

"Why Symbols?" *Ensign,* February 2007, 12.

Widtsoe, John A. "Looking toward the Temple." *Improvement Era,* October 1962, 706.

Woodruff, Wilford. *Discourses of Wilford Woodruff.* Ed. G. Homer Durham. Salt Lake City: Bookcraft, 1969.

Yadin, Yigael. *The Temple Scroll: The Hidden Law of the Dead Sea Sect.* London: Weidenfeld and Nicolson, 1985.

Young, Brigham. *Discourses of Brigham Young.* Ed. John A. Widtsoe. Salt Lake City: Bookcraft, 1998.

# PHOTO CREDITS

All photos © Val Brinkerhoff and used by permission, except as noted.

## PHOTO CREDITS

Page 106  Keystone and handclasp motifs, west side, Salt Lake Temple

Page 116  Gothic-style window, west façade, Kirtland Temple

Page 128  Jacob's Ladder Windows, west side, Mount Timpanogos Utah Temple

Page 138  West window, celestial room, Albuquerque New Mexico Temple

Page 150  Holiness to the Lord inscription, east wall, Salt Lake Temple

Page 158  Eight-pointed star and doorway, south entrance, Sacramento California Temple

Page 170  East doors, Salt Lake Temple

Page 180  Star stone, north wall at sundown, Nauvoo Illinois Temple

Page 190  Northeast window, detail, Winter Quarters Nebraska Temple

Page 198  Jacob's Ladder Window, north side, St. Louis Missouri Temple.

# INDEX

Abraham: participated in temple ordinances, 122; as example of sacrifice, 186–87

Adam: held keys of the First Presidency, 42; was Michael the Archangel, 100; required to participate in sealing ordinances, 100, 102, 104; stands at head of human family, 104; offered sacrifices, 182

Altar, center of sacred actions, 184

Andrus, Milo, on living worthy of revelation, 169

Apostasy: purpose of temple rituals still recognized during, 115; house of Israel existed in state of, 123–24; ordinances and blessings lost through, 125–26

Asay, Carlos E.: on charge to advocate temple activity, 5; on obeying the prophet, 5; on blessings and application of temple attendance, 6; on endowment as symbol of love, 65; on engagement in spiritual war, 134; on protective nature of temple garment, 135; on the temple as the "Lord's University," 173–74

Atonement: and temple ordinances, 13; in effect during premortality, 39, 50; temple is centered on, 47; was predestined, 48–49; redemptive effects of, were guaranteed, 49–50; provided forgiveness of Adam's transgression, 51; belief in, through temple worship, 53; Isaiah sees Savior's, in vision, 53; God's power available through, 87; symbolized in ancient animal sacrifices, 182–83